Agile Project Management with Scrum

Ken Schwaber

PUBLISHED BY
Microsoft Press
A Division of Microsoft Corporation
One Microsoft Way
Redmond, Washington 98052-6399

Library of Congress Cataloging-in-Publication Data
Schwaber, Ken.
     Agile Project Management with Scrum / Ken Schwaber.
          p. cm.
     Includes index.
     ISBN 0-7356-1993-X
     1. Computer software--Development.   2. Project management.   3. Scrum (Computer software development)   I. Title.

     QA76.76.D47S32   2003
     005.1--dc22   2003065178

Printed and bound in the United States of America.

13 14 15   WCT 4 3 2 1 0

Distributed in Canada by H.B. Fenn and Company Ltd.

A CIP catalogue record for this book is available from the British Library.

Microsoft Press books are available through booksellers and distributors worldwide. For further information about international editions, contact your local Microsoft Corporation office or contact Microsoft Press International directly at fax (425) 936-7329. Visit our Web site at www.microsoft.com/mspress. Send comments to *mspinput@microsoft.com*.

Acquisitions Editors: Linda Engelman and Robin Van Steenburgh
Project Editor: Kathleen Atkins
Indexer: Bill Meyers

Body Part No. X10-25679

Dedicated to ScrumMasters

Contents

Foreword

My new boss wasn't being a jerk, but it seemed like it at the time. We were writing new software for use in the company's high-volume call centers. Instead of the 12 months I told him we'd probably need, he had agreed to give me 4 months. We wouldn't necessarily start using the new software in 4 months, but from that point on, all my boss could give me was 30 days' notice of a go-live date. After the first 4 months, I would have to keep the software within 30 days of releasable. My boss understood that not all functionality would be there after 4 months. He just wanted as much as he could get, as fast as he could get it. I needed to find a process that would let us do this. I scoured everything I could find on software development processes, which led me to Scrum and to Ken Schwaber's early writings on it.

In the years since my first Scrum project, I have used Scrum on commercial products, software for internal use, consulting projects, projects with ISO 9001 requirements, and others. Each of these projects was unique, but what they had in common was urgency and criticality. Scrum excels on urgent projects that are critical to an organization. Scrum excels when requirements are unknown, unknowable, or changing. Scrum excels by helping teams excel.

In this book, Ken Schwaber correctly points out that Scrum is hard. It's not hard because of the things you do; it's hard because of the things you don't do. If you're a project manager, you might find some of your conventional tools missing. There are no Gantt charts in Scrum, there's no time reporting, and you don't assign tasks to programmers. Instead you'll learn the few simple rules of Scrum and how to use its frequent inspect-and-adapt cycles to create more valuable software faster.

Ken was there at the beginning of Scrum. Ken, along with Jeff Sutherland, was the original creator of Scrum and has always been its most vocal proponent. In this book, we get to read about many of the Scrum projects Ken has participated in. Ken is a frequent and popular speaker at industry conferences, and if you've ever heard him speak, you know he doesn't pull any punches. This book is the same way: Ken presents both the successes and the failures of past Scrum projects. His goal is to teach us how to make our projects successful, and so he presents examples we can emulate and counterexamples for us to avoid.

This book clearly reflects Ken's experience mentoring Scrum Teams and teaching Certified ScrumMaster courses around the world. Through the many stories in this book, Ken shares with us dozens of the lessons he's learned. This book is an excellent guide for anyone looking to improve how he or she delivers software, and I recommend it highly.

—Mike Cohn
Certified ScrumMaster
Director, Agile Alliance

Foreword: Why Scrum Works

Suppose I'm traveling from Chicago to Boston by airplane. Before and during the flight, the pilot gets instructions from air traffic control. We take off on command and follow the prescribed route. Once we are in the air, computers predict almost to the minute when we will land in Boston. If things change—say the air is bumpy—the pilot must get permission to move to a different altitude. As we approach the airport, the pilot is told what runway to land on and what gate to go to.

If, however, I set out for Boston in a car, I can take whatever route I want, whenever I want. I don't know exactly when I'll get there, and I probably haven't planned what route I'll take or where I'll stop for the night. En route, I follow traffic laws and conventions: I stop at red lights, merge into traffic according to the prevailing customs, and keep my speed consistent with the flow. In an automobile, I am an independent agent, making decisions in my own best interests framed by the rules of the game of driving.

It's amazing to me that thousands upon thousands of people travel by car every day, accomplishing their goals in a framework of simple traffic rules, with no central control or dispatching service. It also amazes me that when I want to ship a package, I can enter a pickup request on the shipper's Web site and a driver will arrive at my door before the time that I specify. The driver isn't dispatched to each house; he or she receives a continually updated list of addresses and deadlines. It's the driver's job to plot a route to get all the packages picked up on time.

As complexity increases, central control and dispatching systems break down. Some might try valiantly to make the control system work by applying more rigor, and indeed that works for a while. But the people who prevail are those who figure out how to change to a system of independent agents operating under an appropriate set of rules. It might work to provide same-day delivery with a dispatch system that plans a driver's route at the beginning of the day. However, it is far more difficult to preplan a pickup route when customers can enter pickup requests at any time. Taxi companies sort things out at a central control center. Some shipping companies send the request to the driver responsible for the area and let the driver determine the best route based on current conditions and other demands.

The more complex the system, the more likely it is that central control systems will break down. This is the reason companies decentralize and governments deregulate—relinquishing control to independent agents is a time-honored approach to dealing with complexity. Scrum travels this well-trodden path by moving control from a central scheduling and dispatching authority to the individual teams doing the work. The more complex the project, the more necessary it becomes to delegate decision making to independent agents who are close to the work.

Another reason that Scrum works is that it dramatically shortens the feedback loop between customer and developer, between wish list and implementation, and between investment and return on investment. Again, complexity plays a role here. When a system is simple, it's not so hard to know in advance what to do. But when we are dealing with a market economy that changes all the time and with technology that won't stand still, learning through short cycles of discovery is the tried-and-true problem-solving approach.

We already know this. We try out various marketing campaigns and discover which approach works. We simulate vehicle behavior during car design to discover the best slope of the hood and best distribution of weight. Virtually all process-improvement programs use some version of the Deming cycle to study a problem, experiment with a solution, measure the results, and adopt proven improvements. We call this fact-based decision making, and we know that it works a lot better than front-end-loaded predictive approaches.

Scrum is built on 30-day learning cycles that prove complete business concepts. If we already know everything and have nothing to discover, perhaps we don't need to use Scrum. If we need to learn, however, Scrum's insistence on delivering complete increments of business value helps us learn rapidly and completely. One of the reasons complete increments are important is that partial answers often fool us into thinking that an approach will work, when in reality, the approach doesn't work upon closer examination. We know that until software is tested, integrated, and released to production, we can't really be sure that it will deliver the intended business value. Scrum forces us to test and integrate our experiments and encourages us to release them to production, so that we have a complete learning cycle every 30 days.

Scrum doesn't focus on delivering just any increment of business value; it focuses on delivering the highest priority business value as defined by the customer (Product Owner). The Product Owner and the Team confer about what that definition is, and then the Team decides what it can do in 30 days to deliver high-priority business value. Thus the short feedback loop becomes a business feedback loop—Scrum tests early and often whether the system being developed will deliver value and exactly what that value will look like. This allows the system to be molded over time to deliver value as it is currently understood, even as it helps to develop a better understanding of that value.

Another reason Scrum works is that it unleashes the brainpower of many minds on a problem. We know that when things go wrong, there are people around who knew there was a problem, but somehow their ideas were overlooked. For example, when the space shuttle disintegrated on reentry, a widely reported interpretation of the causes of the disaster suggests that there were engineers who were well aware that there could be a problem, but they were unable to get their concerns taken seriously. What management system can we use to leverage the experience, ideas, and concerns of the people closest to the work to be done?

According to Gary Convis, president of Toyota Motor Manufacturing Kentucky, the role of managers in a healthy, thriving, work environment is "to shape the organization not through the power of will or dictate, but rather through example, through coaching and through understanding and helping others to achieve their goals."[1]

Scrum turns small teams into managers of their own fate. We know that when we are responsible for choosing our own driving route to Boston, we will find a way to get there. We will detour around construction and avoid rush hour traffic jams, making decisions on the fly, adapting to the independent decisions of all of the other drivers out there. Similarly, Scrum Teams accept a challenge and then figure out how to meet that challenge, detouring around roadblocks in creative ways that could not be planned by a central control and dispatching center.

If teams are of a size that encourages every member to participate, and team members feel like they are in control of their own destiny, the experience, ideas, and concerns of individual members will be leveraged, not squelched. When team members share a common purpose that everyone believes in, they will figure out how to achieve it. When teams understand and commit to delivering business value for their customers, when they are free to figure out how to perform tasks, and when they are given the resources they need, they will succeed.

Gary Convis notes that Toyota's sustainable success comes from an "interlocking set of three underlying elements: the philosophical underpinnings, the managerial culture and the technical tools. The philosophical underpinnings include a joint [worker], customer-first focus, an emphasis on people first, a commitment to continuous improvement.... The managerial culture...is rooted in several factors, including developing and sustaining a sense of trust, a commitment to involving those affected by first, teamwork, equal and fair treatment for all, and finally, fact-based decision making and long-term thinking."[2]

---

1. Gary Convis, "Role of Management in a Lean Manufacturing Environment," in "Learning to Think Lean,"August 2001, SAE International, *http://www.sae.org/topics/leanjul01.htm.*

2. Ibid.

Scrum works for all the same reasons. Its philosophical underpinnings focus on empowering the development team and satisfying customers. Its managerial culture is rooted in helping others achieve their goals. Its technical tools are focused on making fact-based decisions through a learning process. When all of these factors are in place, it's hard for Scrum not to succeed.

—Mary Poppendieck
Poppendieck.LLC

Acknowledgments

Special thanks to my daughter, Carey Schwaber, whose editing turns words into streams, and to Mike Cohn and Mary Poppendieck, for their fine help in keeping this book focused.

Introduction

I offer you Scrum, a most perplexing and paradoxical process for managing complex projects. On one hand, Scrum is disarmingly simple. The process, its practices, its artifacts, and its rules are few, straightforward, and easy to learn. In 2001, Mike Beedle and I wrote a short, straightforward book describing Scrum: *Agile Software Development with Scrum* (Prentice Hall). On the other hand, Scrum's simplicity can be deceptive. Scrum is not a prescriptive process; it doesn't describe what to do in every circumstance. Scrum is used for complex work in which it is impossible to predict everything that will occur. Accordingly, Scrum simply offers a framework and set of practices that keep everything visible. This allows Scrum's practitioners to know exactly what's going on and to make on-the-spot adjustments to keep the project moving toward the desired goals.

Common sense is a combination of experience, training, humility, wit, and intelligence. People employing Scrum apply common sense every time they find the work is veering off the path leading to the desired results. Yet most of us are so used to using prescriptive processes—those that say "do this, then do that, and then do this"—that we have learned to disregard our common sense and instead await instructions.

I wrote this book to help people understand how to use Scrum as they work on complex problems. Instead of further describing the framework and practices of Scrum, I offer a number of case studies in which people use Scrum to solve complex problems and perform complex work. In some of these case studies, people use Scrum correctly and the project in question ends up achieving their goals. In other case studies, people struggle with Scrum and their projects are less successful. These are people to whom Scrum is not intuitive. I've worked to understand how this can be possible. After all, Scrum is a very simple process for managing complex projects. Compared to many traditional approaches to project management, Scrum is almost effortless. Or at least I used to think it was.

Most people responsible for managing projects have been taught a deterministic approach to project management that uses detailed plans, Gantt charts, and work schedules. Scrum is the exact opposite. Unlike these tools, which practically fight against a project's natural momentum, Scrum shows management how to guide a project along its optimal course, which unfolds as the project proceeds. I've heard that traveling along a learning curve starts from a point where you have to think everything through step by step and ends at a point where you can perform the work in question unconsciously. This is particularly true of Scrum because those steeped in traditional management practices have to unlearn many of them.

I recently helped a software development company adopt Scrum. Initially, the company had planned for two releases over the next 12 months. Because of its success in using Scrum, however, most of the functionality from the two releases was ready within 5 months. But when I visited the engineering organization, the staff was working weekends and nights to put even more functionality into the release. Even though the engineers had been wildly successful, marketing still was berating them for not delivering enough and living up to "commitments." The engineers were feeling guilty for not doing everything that marketing said was necessary, and they were ruining their personal lives to try to do everything marketing requested. This pathology had persisted despite the fact that the engineers had already accomplished the work involved in two releases in the time usually allotted for one. Old habits die hard.

Another change that Scrum engenders can best be described by thinking of how a house is built. The buyer of the house cannot move into the house until the entire house is completed. Suppose that there were an incremental, iterative approach for home construction. Suppose that using this approach, houses were built room by room. The plumbing, electrical, and infrastructure would be built in the first room and then extended to each room as it was constructed. Buyers could move in as soon as they had decided that enough rooms had been completed. Then additional rooms could be constructed depending on the needs of the buyer. Scrum lets buyers have software built in this fashion. While the infrastructure is deployed, pieces of functionality are delivered to buyers so that their organizations can start using parts of the system early in the development cycle. As the system is experienced, the buyer can determine which parts of the system will be constructed in what order and use these parts as they are completed. Buyers might even choose not to have the entire system built if they are satisfied with only a subset of the total functionality they'd initially envisioned.

I used to teach people the theory, practices, and rules of Scrum. Now I teach them what Scrum feels like as it is implemented. I teach them how to recognize when things are going right and when they are going wrong. I provide exercises and discussions that let them experience the epiphanies so that they know what Scrum should feel like. Just as you don't really know what it's like to be someone else until you've walked however many miles in his or her shoes, you might not fully understand Scrum until you implement it yourself. But as you read this book, you will begin to understand what Scrum feels like and how you might feel using Scrum in your organization.

How should you read this book, which is in essence a book of case studies about Scrum? I've provided some of the background for each story, described how Scrum was used in that situation, and presented some of the lessons that can be learned from the way Scrum was used. The case studies are organized into topical chapters, through which you should feel free to browse. The chapter topics are Chapter 1, "Backdrop: The Science of Scrum; Chapter 2, "New Management Responsibilities"; Chapter 3, "The ScrumMaster"; Chapter 4, "Bringing Order from Chaos"; Chapter 5, "The Product Owner"; Chapter 6, "Planning a Scrum Project"; Chapter 7, "Project Reporting"; Chapter 8, "The Team"; and Chapter 9, "Scaling Projects Using Scrum." Sometimes I indicate that the background for a story has been provided in a previous chapter.

Appendix A, "Rules," lists the rules that are used in various Scrum practices and meetings. These rules hold Scrum together. If you are familiar with Scrum but you come across terms that you do not fully understand, you should look them up in Appendix B, "Definitions." If you are unfamiliar with Scrum, you should read Chapter 1, "Backdrop: The Science of Scrum," for a recap of Scrum theory, flow, practices, artifacts, roles, and meetings. Appendix C, "Resources," provides a list of resources that you might want to access to get a deeper understanding of Scrum.

Appendix D, "Fixed-Price, Fixed-Date Contracts," and Appendix E, "Capability Maturity Model," are the odd ducks of this book. They contain material that might help you use Scrum in rather unique circumstances that aren't described in the case studies that constitute the body of this book.

1

Backdrop: The Science of Scrum

Software development is a complex endeavor. Of course, this news isn't very surprising because the universe is full of complexity. Most complexities we don't know about, and others we are content to leave unexamined. Some—like the complex process by which pressure turns coal into diamonds—take care of themselves. Others—for example, commuting to work every day—can tolerate some imprecision. However, it is impossible to ignore complexity in software development. Its results are ephemeral, consisting merely of signals that control machines. The software development process is entirely intellectual, and all of its intermediate products are marginal representations of the thoughts involved. The materials that we use to create the end product are extremely volatile: user requirements for a program the users have yet to see, the interoperation of other programs' signals with the program in question, and the interaction of the most complex organisms on the planet—people.

This book addresses the extraordinarily difficult process of creating software. In this chapter, I'll summarize a process for increasing the probability of successfully developing software. This process, Scrum, is devised specifically to wrest usable products from complex problems. It has been used successfully on thousands of projects in hundreds of organizations over the last 10 years. It is based in industrial process control theory, which employs mechanisms such as self-organization and emergence.

This book is about the ScrumMaster, the Scrum project manager who heads the Scrum project. The ScrumMaster provides leadership, guidance, and coaching. The ScrumMaster is responsible for teaching others how to use the Scrum process to deal with every new complexity encountered during a project. Because of the nature of software development, there is no shortage of complexities, and there is no way to resolve them without hard work, intelligence, and courage.

This chapter describes how empirical processes are used to control complex processes and how Scrum employs these empirical processes to control software development projects. When I say that Scrum helps control a software development project, I don't mean that it ensures that the project will go exactly as expected, yielding results identical to those that were predicted. Rather, I mean that Scrum controls the process of software development to guide work toward the most valuable outcome possible.

Empirical Process Control

Complex problems are those that behave unpredictably. Not only are these problems unpredictable, but even the ways in which they will prove unpredictable are impossible to predict. To put that another way, a statistical sample of the operation of these processes will never yield meaningful insight into their underlying mathematical model, and attempts to create a sample can only be made by summarizing their operation to such a degree of coarseness as to be irrelevant to those trying to understand or manage these processes.

Much of our society is based on processes that work only because their degree of imprecision is acceptable. Wheels wobble, cylinders shake, and brakes jitter, but this all occurs at a level that doesn't meaningfully impede our use of a car. When we build cars, we fit parts together with a degree of precision fit for their intended purpose. We can manage many processes because the accuracy of the results is limited by our physical perceptions. For example, when I build a cabinet, I need only cut and join the materials with enough precision to make them acceptable to the human eye; if I were aiming only for functionality, I could be far less precise.

What happens when we are building something that requires a degree of precision higher than that obtainable through averaging? What happens if any process that we devise for building cars is too imprecise for our customers, and we need to increase the level of precision? In those cases, we have to guide the process step by step, ensuring that the process converges on an acceptable degree of precision. In cases where convergence doesn't occur, we have to make adaptations to bring the process back into the range of acceptable precision levels. Laying out a process that repeatably will produce acceptable quality output is called *defined process control*. When defined process control cannot be achieved because of the complexity of the intermediate activities, something called *empirical process control* has to be employed.

*It is typical to adopt the defined (theoretical) modeling
approach when the underlying mechanisms by which a process
operates are reasonably well understood. When the process is
too complicated for the defined approach, the empirical
approach is the appropriate choice.*

—*B. A. Ogunnaike and W. H. Ray,*
Process Dynamics, Modeling, and Control[1]

We use defined processes whenever possible because with them we can
crank up unattended production to such a quantity that the output can be
priced as a commodity. However, if the commodity is of such unacceptable
quality as to be unusable, the rework is too great to make the price acceptable,
or the cost of unacceptably low yields is too high, we have to turn to and accept
the higher costs of empirical process control. In the long run, making successful
products the first time using empirical process control turns out to be much
cheaper than reworking unsuccessful products using defined process control.
There are three legs that hold up every implementation of empirical process
control: *visibility*, *inspection*, and *adaptation*. Visibility means that those
aspects of the process that affect the outcome must be visible to those controlling the process. Not only must these aspects be visible, but what is visible must
also be true. There is no room for deceiving appearances in empirical process
control. What does it mean, for example, when someone says that certain functionality is labeled "done"? In software development, asserting that functionality
is done might lead someone to assume that it is cleanly coded, refactored, unit-
tested, built, and acceptance-tested. Someone else might assume that the code
has only been built. It doesn't matter whether it is visible that this functionality
is done if no one can agree what the word "done" means.

The second leg is inspection. The various aspects of the process must be
inspected frequently enough that unacceptable variances in the process can be
detected. The frequency of inspection has to take into consideration that processes are changed by the very act of inspection. Interestingly, the required frequency of inspection often exceeds the tolerance to inspection of the process.
Fortunately, this isn't usually true in software development. The other factor in
inspection is the inspector, who must possess the skills to assess what he or she
is inspecting.

The third leg of empirical process control is adaptation. If the inspector
determines from the inspection that one or more aspects of the process are outside acceptable limits and that the resulting product will be unacceptable, the

---

1. (Oxford University Press, 1992), p. 364.

inspector must adjust the process or the material being processed. The adjustment must be made as quickly as possible to minimize further deviation.

Let's take code review as an example of an empirical process control. The code is reviewed against coding standards and industry best practices. Everyone involved in the review fully and mutually understands these standards and best practices. The code review occurs whenever someone feels that a section of code or code representing a piece of functionality is complete. The most experienced developers review the code, and their comments and suggestions lead to the developer adjusting his or her code.

Complex Software Development

When I develop software, I build a logical set of instructions that send signals that control a machine in its interactions with other machines, humans, or nature. The level of precision required for successful software ranges from the incredible to the truly daunting. Anything can be complex. When complex things interact, the level of complexity goes through the roof. I've limited my enumeration of complexity in software development to the three most significant dimensions: requirements, technology, and people.

It is possible to have simple software requirements. A single customer who is the only person who will use the system can spend enough time with the developer that the two can agree exactly what to build. Assuming that this customer dies immediately after imparting his or her requirements, the requirements will remain constant, and there will be no changes, revisions, or last-minute modifications. More commonly, there are many *stakeholders* (those with an interest in the software and how it works) who have different needs and whose needs frequently change and are difficult to articulate. In most cases, these customers only really start to understand what they want when they are provided with someone else's impression of what they want. Theirs are complex requirements because their requirements are not only ambiguous, but also constantly changing.

Simple technology exists, but it is rarely used in software development. One might define software development projects as the application of advanced, often unreliable technology to solve business problems and achieve competitive advantage. To compound the complexity of technology, more than one piece is usually employed, and the interfaces of the many are far more complex than the complexity within any single piece.

In Figure 1-1, the vertical axis traces requirements complexity, and the horizontal axis traces technology complexity. The intersection of these two kinds of complexity defines the total level of complexity of the project. Almost all of today's software development projects are complex. Those that are chaotic are unworkable, and some of their complexities must be resolved before work can progress.

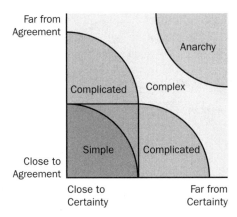

Figure 1-1   Complexity assessment graph

The third dimension of complexity is the people developing the software. They all have different skills, intelligence levels, experience, viewpoints, attitudes, and prejudices. Every morning, each wakes up in a different mood than the day before, depending on his or her sleep, health, weather, neighbors, and families. These people then start to work together, and the complexity level goes through the roof. Taking into account this last dimension—people—in addition to technology and requirements, I believe that the last "simple" project occurred in 1969, when one person from order processing at Sears Roebuck asked me to sort some cards and generate a report on an IBM 360/20. Since then, things have only gotten messier. Scrum addresses the complexity of software development projects by implementing the inspection, adaptation, and visibility requirements of empirical process control with a set of simple practices and rules, which are described in the following sections.

The Skeleton and Heart of Scrum

Scrum hangs all of its practices on an iterative, incremental process skeleton. Scrum's skeleton is shown in Figure 1-2. The lower circle represents an iteration of development activities that occur one after another. The output of each iteration is an increment of product. The upper circle represents the daily inspection that occurs during the iteration, in which the individual team members meet to inspect each others' activities and make appropriate adaptations. Driving the iteration is a list of requirements. This cycle repeats until the project is no longer funded.

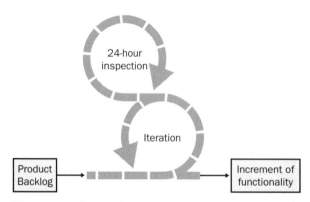

Figure 1-2 Scrum skeleton

The skeleton operates this way: At the start of an iteration, the team reviews what it must do. It then selects what it believes it can turn into an increment of potentially shippable functionality by the end of the iteration. The team is then left alone to make its best effort for the rest of the iteration. At the end of the iteration, the team presents the increment of functionality it built so that the stakeholders can inspect the functionality and timely adaptations to the project can be made.

The heart of Scrum lies in the iteration. The team takes a look at the requirements, considers the available technology, and evaluates its own skills and capabilities. It then collectively determines how to build the functionality, modifying its approach daily as it encounters new complexities, difficulties, and surprises. The team figures out what needs to be done and selects the best way to do it. This creative process is the heart of the Scrum's productivity.

Scrum implements this iterative, incremental skeleton through three roles. I'll provide a quick overview of these people operating within the Scrum process. Then I'll describe the Scrum process flow and its artifacts. Appendix A, "Rules," and Appendix B, "Definitions," provide a list of rules as well as Scrum definitions that can be referred to as you read this book. More detailed information about Scrum can be found in Appendix C, "Resources," and in Ken Schwaber and Mike Beedle's, *Agile Software Development with Scrum* (Prentice Hall, 2002).

Scrum Roles

There are only three Scrum roles: the Product Owner, the Team, and the Scrum-Master. All management responsibilities in a project are divided among these three roles. The Product Owner is responsible for representing the interests of everyone with a stake in the project and its resulting system. The Product Owner achieves initial and ongoing funding for the project by creating the project's initial overall requirements, return on investment (ROI) objectives, and release plans. The list of requirements is called the Product Backlog. The Product Owner is responsible for using the Product Backlog to ensure that the most valuable functionality is produced first and built upon; this is achieved by frequently prioritizing the Product Backlog to queue up the most valuable requirements for the next iteration. The Team is responsible for developing functionality. Teams are self-managing, self-organizing, and cross-functional, and they are responsible for figuring out how to turn Product Backlog into an increment of functionality within an iteration and managing their own work to do so. Team members are collectively responsible for the success of each iteration and of the project as a whole. The ScrumMaster is responsible for the Scrum process, for teaching Scrum to everyone involved in the project, for implementing Scrum so that it fits within an organization's culture and still delivers the expected benefits, and for ensuring that everyone follows Scrum rules and practices.

The people who fill these roles are those who have committed to the project. Others might be interested in the project, but they aren't on the hook. Scrum makes a clear distinction between these two groups and ensures that those who are responsible for the project have the authority to do what is necessary for its success and that those who aren't responsible can't interfere unnecesarily. Throughout this book, I refer to these people as "pigs" and "chickens," respectively. These names come from an old joke: A chicken and a pig are walking down the road. The chicken says to the pig, "Do you want to open a restaurant with me?" The pig considers the question and replies, "Yes, I'd like that. What do you want to call the restaurant?" The chicken replies, "Ham and Eggs!" The pig stops, pauses, and replies, "On second thought, I don't think I want to open a restaurant with you. I'd be committed, but you'd only be involved."

This distinction is important in Scrum and is relevant to Scrum's insistence upon total visibility. It should always be clear who is on the hook and who is just a kibitzer. Who is responsible for the ROI, and who has a stake in the ROI but isn't accountable? Who has to turn difficult technology into functionality, and who is a troublesome "devil's advocate"? The rules of Scrum distinguish between the chickens and the pigs to increase productivity, create momentum, and put an end to floundering.

Scrum Flow

A Scrum project starts with a vision of the system to be developed. The vision might be vague at first, perhaps stated in market terms rather than system terms, but it will become clearer as the project moves forward. The Product Owner is responsible to those funding the project for delivering the vision in a manner that maximizes their ROI. The Product Owner formulates a plan for doing so that includes a Product Backlog. The Product Backlog is a list of functional and nonfunctional requirements that, when turned into functionality, will deliver this vision. The Product Backlog is prioritized so that the items most likely to generate value are top priority and is divided into proposed releases. The prioritized Product Backlog is a starting point, and the contents, priorities, and grouping of the Product Backlog into releases usually changes the moment the project starts—as should be expected. Changes in the Product Backlog reflect changing business requirements and how quickly or slowly the Team can transform Product Backlog into functionality.

All work is done in Sprints. Each Sprint is an iteration of 30 consecutive calendar days. Each Sprint is initiated with a Sprint planning meeting, where the Product Owner and Team get together to collaborate about what will be done for the next Sprint. Selecting from the highest priority Product Backlog, the Product Owner tells the Team what is desired, and the Team tells the Product Owner how much of what is desired it believes it can turn into functionality over the next Sprint. Sprint planning meetings cannot last longer than eight hours—that is, they are time-boxed to avoid too much hand-wringing about what is possible. The goal is to get to work, not to think about working.

The Sprint planning meeting has two parts. The first four hours are spent with the Product Owner presenting the highest priority Product Backlog to the Team. The Team questions him or her about the content, purpose, meaning, and intentions of the Product Backlog. When the Team knows enough, but before the first four hours elapses, the Team selects as much Product Backlog as it believes it can turn into a completed increment of potentially shippable product functionality by the end of the Sprint. The Team commits to the Product Owner that it will do its best. During the second four hours of the Sprint planning meeting, the Team plans out the Sprint. Because the Team is responsible for managing its own work, it needs a tentative plan to start the Sprint. The tasks that compose this plan are placed in a Sprint Backlog; the tasks in the Sprint Backlog emerge as the Sprint evolves. At the start of the second four-hour period of the Sprint planning meeting, the Sprint has started, and the clock is ticking toward the 30-day Sprint time-box.

Every day, the team gets together for a 15-minute meeting called a Daily Scrum. At the Daily Scrum, each Team member answers three questions: What have you done on this project since the last Daily Scrum meeting? What do you plan on doing on this project between now and the next Daily Scrum meeting? What impediments stand in the way of you meeting your commitments to this Sprint and this project? The purpose of the meeting is to synchronize the work of all Team members daily and to schedule any meetings that the Team needs to forward its progress.

At the end of the Sprint, a Sprint review meeting is held. This is a four-hour, time-boxed meeting at which the Team presents what was developed during the Sprint to the Product Owner and any other stakeholders who want to attend. This informal meeting at which the functionality is presented is intended to bring people together and help them collaboratively determined what the Team should do next. After the Sprint review and prior to the next Sprint planning meeting, the ScrumMaster holds a Sprint retrospective meeting with the Team. At this three-hour, time-boxed meeting, the ScrumMaster encourages the Team to revise, within the Scrum process framework and practices, its development process to make it more effective and enjoyable for the next Sprint. Together, the Sprint planning meeting, the Daily Scrum, the Sprint review, and the Sprint retrospective constitute the empirical inspection and adaptation practices of Scrum. Take a look at Figure 1-3 to see a diagram of the Scrum process.

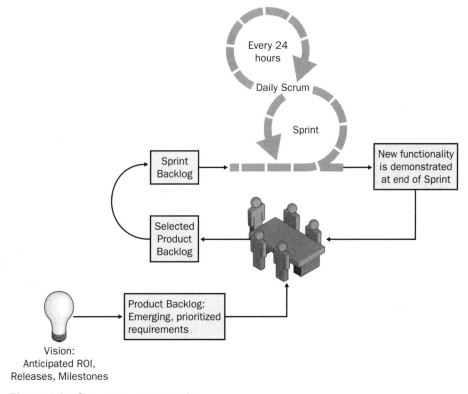

Figure 1-3   Scrum process overview

Scrum Artifacts

Scrum introduces a few new artifacts. These are used throughout the Scrum process and are described in the following sections.

Product Backlog

The requirements for the system or product being developed by the project(s) are listed in the Product Backlog. The Product Owner is responsible for the contents, prioritization, and availability of the Product Backlog. The Product Backlog is never complete, and the Product Backlog used in the project plan is merely an initial estimate of the requirements. The Product Backlog evolves as the product and the environment in which it will be used evolves. The Product Backlog is dynamic; management constantly changes it to identify what the product needs to be appropriate, competitive, and useful. As long as a product exists, the Product Backlog also exists. An example of Product Backlog maintained on the Scrum Product Management tool, based in a spreadsheet, is shown in Figure 1-4.

Backlog Description	Initial Estimate	Adjust-ment Factor	Adjusted Estimate	work remaining until completion						
				1	2	3	4	5	6	7
Title Import				256	209	193	140	140	140	140
Project selection or new	3	0.2	3.6	3.6	0	0	0	0	0	0
Template backlog for new projects	2	0.2	2.4	2.4	0	0	0	0	0	0
Create product backlog worksheet with formatting	3	0.2	3.6	3.6	0	0	0	0	0	0
Create sprint backlog worksheet with formatting	3	0.2	3.6	3.6	0	0	0	0	0	0
Display tree view of product backlog, releases, sprints	2	0.2	2.4	2.4	0	0	0	0	0	0
Sprint-1	13	0.2	15.6	16	0	0	0	0	0	0
Create a new window containing product backlog template	3	0.2	3.6	3.6	3.6	0	0	0	0	0
Create a new window containing sprint backlog template	2	0.2	2.4	2.4	2.4	0	0	0	0	0
Burndown window of product backlog	5	0.2	6	6	6	0	0	0	0	0
Burndown window of sprint backlog	1	0.2	1.2	1.2	1.2	0	0	0	0	0
Display tree view of product backlog, releases, prints	2	0.2	2.4	2.4	2.4	0	0	0	0	0
Display burndown for selected sprint or release	3	0.2	3.6	3.6	3.6	0	0	0	0	0
Sprint-2	16	0.2	19.2	19	19	1.2	0	0	0	0
Automatic recalculating of values and totals	3	0.2	3.6	3.6	3.6	3.6	0	0	0	0
As changes are made to backlog in secondary window, update burndown graph on main page	2	0.2	2.4	2.4	2.4	2.4	0	0	0	0
Hide/automatic redisplay of burndown window	3	0.2	3.6	3.6	3.6	3.6	0	0	0	0
Insert Sprint capability ... adds summing Sprint row	2	0.2	2.4	2.4	2.4	2.4	0	0	0	0
Insert Release capability ... adds summary row for backlog in Sprint	1	0.2	1.2	1.2	1.2	1.2	0	0	0	0
Owner/assigned capability and columns optional	2	0.2	2.4	2.4	2.4	2.4	0	0	0	0
Print burndown graphs	1	0.2	1.2	1.2	1.2	1.2	0	0	0	0
Sprint-3	14	0.2	16.8	17	17	17	0	0	0	0
Duplicate incomplete backlog without affecting totals	5	0.2	6	6	6	6	6	6	6	6
Note capability	6	0.2	7.2	7.2	7.2	7.2	7.2	7.2	7.2	7.2
What-if release capability on burndown graph	15	0.2	18	18	18	18	18	18	18	18
Trend capability on burndown server	2	0.2	2.4	2.4	2.4	2.4	2.4	2.4	2.4	2.4
Publish facility for entire project, publishing it as HTML web pages	11	0.2	13.2	0	0	13	13	13	13	13
Future Sprints	39	0.2	46.8	34	34	47	47	47	47	47
Release-1				85	70	65	47	47	47	47

Figure 1-4   Product Backlog

This spreadsheet is the March 2003 Product Backlog for a project for developing the Scrum Project Management software. I was the Product Owner. The rows are the Product Backlog items, separated by Sprint and Release sub-headings. For instance, all of the rows above Sprint 1 represent tasks that were worked on in that Sprint. The rows between the Sprint 1 and Sprint 2 subhead-ings were done in Sprint 2. Notice that the row Display Tree View Of Product Backlog, Releases, Sprints is duplicated in Sprint 1 and Sprint 2. This is because row 10 wasn't completed in Sprint 1, so it was moved down to the Sprint 2 for completion. If I decided that it was lower priority after Sprint 1, I could have moved it even lower in the priority list.

The first four columns are the Product Backlog item name, the initial esti-mate, the complexity factor, and the adjusted estimate. The complexity factor increases the estimate due to project characteristics that reduce the productivity of the Team. The remaining columns represent the Sprints during which the Product Backlog is developed. When the Product Backlog is first thought of and entered, its estimated work is placed into the column of the Sprint that is going on at that time. The developers and I devised most of the backlog items shown before starting this project. The sole exception is row 31 (Publish Facility For Entire Project, Publishing It As HTML Web Pages), which I didn't think of until Sprint 3.

A *burndown chart* shows the amount of work remaining across time. The burndown chart is an excellent way of visualizing the correlation between the amount of work remaining at any point in time and the progress of the project Team(s) in reducing this work. The intersection of a trend line for work remain-ing and the horizontal axis indicates the most probable completion of work at that point in time. A burndown chart reflecting this is shown in Figure 1-5. This allows me to "what if" the project by adding and removing functionality from the release to get a more acceptable date or extend the date to include more functionality. The burndown chart is the collision of reality (work done and how fast it's being done) with what is planned, or hoped for.

The items in the Product Backlog for future Sprints are quite coarse-grained. I haven't had the Team start work on these items, so I haven't expended the time to analyze and more finely estimate them. Similarly, there are plenty more requirements for this product. They just haven't been thought through. When I have the time or inclination to start development again, I'll define more Product Backlog items. This is an example of the requirements for the product emerging. I can defer building an inventory of Product Backlog until I am ready to engage a Team to convert it to functionality.

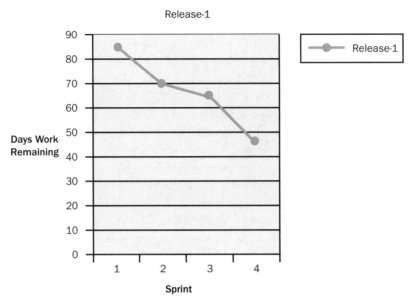

Figure 1-5   Burndown chart

Sprint Backlog

The Sprint Backlog defines the work, or tasks, that a Team defines for turning the Product Backlog it selected for that Sprint into an increment of potentially shippable product functionality. The Team compiles an initial list of these tasks in the second part of the Sprint planning meeting. Tasks should be divided so that each takes roughly 4 to 16 hours to finish. Tasks longer than 4 to 16 hours are considered mere placeholders for tasks that haven't yet been appropriately defined. Only the Team can change the Sprint Backlog. The Sprint Backlog is a highly visible, real-time picture of the work that the Team plans to accomplish during the Sprint. An example Sprint Backlog is shown in Figure 1-6. The rows represent Sprint Backlog tasks; the columns represent the 30 days in the Sprint. Once a task is defined, the estimated number of hours remaining to complete the task is placed in the intersection of the task and the Sprint day by the person working on the task.

Increment of Potentially Shippable Product Functionality

Scrum requires Teams to build an increment of product functionality every Sprint. This increment must be potentially shippable, because the Product Owner might choose to immediately implement the functionality. This requires that the increment consist of thoroughly tested, well-structured, and well-written code that has been built into an executable and that the user operation of the functionality is documented, either in Help files or in user documentation. This is the definition of a "done" increment.

Task Description	Originator	Responsible	Status (Not Started/In Progress/ Completed)	1	2	3	4	5	6	7	8	9	10	11	12
Meet to discuss the goals and features for Sprint 3-6	Danielle	Danielle/Sue	Completed	20	0	0	0	0	0	0	0	0	0	0	0
Move Calculations out of Crystal Reports	Jim	Allen	Not Started	8	8	8	8	8	8	8	8	8	8	8	8
Get KEG Data		Tom	Completed	12	0	0	0	0	0	0	0	0	0	0	0
Analyse KEG Data - Title		George	In Progress	24	24	24	24	12	10	10	10	10	10	10	10
Analyse KEG Data - Parcel		Tim	Completed	12	12	12	12	12	4	4	4	0	0	0	0
Analyse KEG Data - Encumbrance		Josh	In Progress							12	10	10	10	10	10
Analyse KEG Data - Contact		Danielle	In Progress	24	24	24	24	12	10	8	6	6	6	6	6
Analyse KEG Data - Facilities		Allen	In Progress	24	24	24	24	12	10	10	10	10	10	10	10
Define & build Database		Barry/Dave	In Progress	80	80	80	80	80	80	60	60	60	60	60	60
Validate the size of the KEG database		Tim	Not Started												
Look at KEG Data on the G:\		Dave	In Progress	3	3	3	3	3	3	3	3	3	3	3	3
Confirm agreement with KEG		Sue	Not Started												
Confirm KEG Staff Availablity		Tom	Not Started	1	1	1	1	1	1	1	1	1	1	1	1
Switch JDK to 1.3.1. Run all tests.		Allen	Not Started	8	8	8	8	8	8	8	8	8	8	8	8
Store PDF files in a structure		Jacquie	Completed	8	0	0	0	0	0	0	0	0	0	0	0
TopLink. Cannot get rid of netscape parser		Richard	Comleted	4	0	0	0	0	0	0	0	0	0	0	0
Buld test data repository		Barry	In Progress	10	10	10	10	10	10	10	10	8	8	8	8
Move application and database to Qual (incl Crystal)		Richard	Completed	4	4	4	4	4	4	4	0	0	0	0	0
Set up Crystal environment		Josh	Completed	2	2	2	2	1	1	1	0	0	0	0	0
Test App in Qual		Sue	In Progress												20
Defining sprint goal required for solution in 2002		Lynne	In Progress	40	40	40	40	40	40	40	38	38	38	38	38
Reference tables for import process		Josh	In Progress												
Build standard import exception process		Josh	In Progress									12	12	12	10
Handle multiple file imports on same page		Jacquie	Disregarded												
Migrate CruiseControl Servlet to iWS 6.0 (landcc_7101) server		Allen	Not Started	4	4	4	4	4	4	4	4	4	4	4	4
Create web server for Qual on PF1D8		Allen	Completed	1	0	0	0	0	0	0	0	0	0	0	0
LTCS Disk		Danielle/ George	In Progress	12	12	12	12	8	8	8	8	8	8	8	8
Follow thru with questions about KEG data to Sue/Tom, re: Keg, LTO	Jacquie	Danielle	Completed	10	10	10	10	10	8	8	0	0	0	0	0
Map KEG data to Active Tables - see also #14	Jacquie	Jacquie/Allen	In Progress	50	50	50	50	50	50	50	50	50	50	50	50
Preparer SQL to import from KEG tables to Active Tables	Jacquie	George	In Progress	25	25	25	25	25	25	25	25	25	25	25	25

(Hours of work remaining unt...)

Figure 1-6   Sprint Backlog

If the product increment that is created during the Sprint has a more exacting use, the development organization usually defines the additional product requirements as standards or conventions. For example, the Food and Drug Administration (FDA) approves all products that will be used in life-critical circumstances in healthcare settings. As part of the approval process, the FDA checks that the product requirements are adequate and complete and that the requirements can be directly traced to the product. For each increment of FDA life-critical products to be potentially shippable, these additional facets of the product must also be developed—so that each increment of the product is potentially ready for FDA approval.

Summary

There you have it: the theory, the skeleton, the heart, the roles, the flow, and the artifacts of Scrum. For more of the how, why, and what of Scrum, refer to the Appendixes for more resources, a glossary of terms, and the Scrum rules. But remember that just as my bike trips in eastern Massachusetts don't qualify me for the Tour de France, the knowledge I've imparted in this chapter doesn't qualify you to manage a project with Scrum. For this, you need some practice and some understanding of Scrum being applied in real situations. That's what the next chapters are about—the practice of Scrum.

2

New Management Responsibilities

As you saw in Chapter 1, in Scrum, the world is divided into pigs and chickens. Pigs are those who are committed to a project, those who have "skin in the game." Chickens are the spectators. This analogy can help us to understand the three management roles in Scrum; all three roles are "pig" roles. These roles—Product Owner, ScrumMaster, and Team—are clear and easy to understand. Although it might seem counterintuitive that Teams are managers, one of the central tenets of Scrum is that Teams handle their own management. All other managers in an organization are chickens, who might be interested in the project and who might have a strong vested interest in its success, but who have to work through the pigs. Chickens have no direct authority over the project's execution or progress.

The good news is that Scrum greatly simplifies issues of accountability and authority for Scrum's management. The bad news is that the Scrum management roles are difficult to play. Managing complex work is never easy, and Scrum never gives its managers a break. Scrum practices regularly make visible a project's progress, problems, and sociology. Scrum management is responsible for inspecting the aspects of the project that Scrum makes visible and adapting accordingly.

In this chapter, I'll present these three Scrum management roles and show how they work. In later chapters, I'll talk about people who filled these roles—with varying degrees of success.

The ScrumMaster at MetaEco

The ScrumMaster fills the position normally occupied by the project manager. I've taken the liberty of redefining this role. While the traditional project manager is responsible for defining and managing the work, the ScrumMaster is responsible for managing the Scrum process. To put it simply, ScrumMasters make Scrum work.

The Scrum process defines practices, meetings, artifacts, and terminology. The ScrumMaster is responsible for knowing these and knowing how to apply them correctly. Scrum can be applied incorrectly, as we will see. But because the ScrumMaster has a clear understanding of how Scrum works and has experience applying Scrum, the ScrumMaster knows how to guide a Scrum project through the shoals of complexity.

Like sheep in an open field, individuals in a project tend to stray. The ScrumMaster's job is to keep the flock together. In fact, I often compare a ScrumMaster to a sheepdog, responsible for keeping the flock together and the wolves away.

The Situation at MetaEco

MetaEco develops and sells code generation software. It owns a library of object patterns that describe various business enterprises. Customers customize the objects in their business's pattern to describe their unique business model and to generate applications for their business. MetaEco, a three-year-old company, had enjoyed a steady revenue stream from its first customer. However, this customer had just been acquired by a competitor and was unlikely to renew its contract.

MetaEco was in a tight spot: it had been spending more money than it took in, and its product was complex and expensive. MetaEco's primary costs were new product development and development of customized solutions based on the core product. Every prospect required a customization of the product to its needs before moving forward. Making this initial investment was costly for MetaEco, and not enough prospects were becoming paying customers to make up for that cost.

The ScrumMaster in Action

Tom, the MetaEco CTO, asked me to train the development staff in Scrum. Tom decided that he needed to be ScrumMaster because of his technical skills and his determination to keep MetaEco on track. Tom and I formed teams charged with enhancing the current product and building a prototype for a very important prospect, a news organization. The prospective customer had said that it would consider funding a long-term partnership if the prototype was to its liking.

Tom did a great job of reinforcing the Scrum teachings of cross-functional teams, cajoling and educating each team when it reverted to design sessions that weren't in line with that Sprint's goal. Tom also worked hard to protect the teams from outside interference. Tom's biggest challenge in this area turned out to be his mentor, Paul, who was MetaEco's new CEO. Paul served as the company's chief salesman, and was usually on the road drumming up business. The two men were positioned to serve as counterpoints to one another. Tom brought stability and focus to the teams so that they could rapidly build demonstrable products. Paul worked to find money to keep the company afloat. Often, Paul would have to commit to a proof of concept before the prospects were willing to take the next step. Tom discovered Paul redirecting the team members from their Sprint work more than once. Paul would ask a key developer to tweak the product and buff it up for presentation to a prospect. Although each customization could be completed in only three or four days, these interruptions shattered a team's focus and slashed away at its productivity.

Paul argued that all he needed were a couple more prospects becoming customers to generate much-needed revenues. To make the prospects customers, he required customized prototypes. Tom argued that Paul, as Product Owner, had already prioritized work the team had to complete to finalize contracts with the important prospective customer. Staffing had been reduced so that the new organization's project and other customizations couldn't be completed simultaneously. Tom reminded Paul that his opportunity to direct the team's work was the Sprint planning meeting. If he wanted another prototype built in parallel with the news organization's project, he could choose to do so at that time and visibly accept the consequences of slowing progress on the news organization's project. Or he could choose to prioritize another prospect above that one.

Paul was in a bind. He didn't want to miss out on any opportunities, but he also didn't want to screw up the news organization's project. Tom was sympathetic, but he also understood that if he didn't stand firm and stick to the rules of Scrum, nothing would get done. Finally Paul said, "All right! I don't like the Scrum rules, but I understand them. Now that I know the rules, I'll follow them. But you'd better be willing to turn on a dime at the Sprint planning meeting!"

The ScrumMaster's Value

Let's see how Tom as ScrumMaster added value to MetaEco. The sales and marketing departments are often at odds with the development organization. Sales and marketing want quick responses to every opportunity that comes knocking. Developers need to focus on producing the product. The chaos in a company is often caused by an inability to resolve these conflicting needs.

Scrum strikes a balance between the two through the use of 30-day Sprints. The development organization will do whatever is needed every Sprint, addressing whatever is deemed the top priority for that Sprint. However, everyone else must leave the developers alone to work.

As ScrumMaster, Tom was able to cite two rules to help his team and ultimately MetaEco. First, he highlighted the Scrum rule banning interference during the Sprint. Then he reminded Paul of the Scrum rule that allows a team to be redirected to higher priority work at the Sprint planning meeting. The first rule protected his team and its work, and the second rule reassured Paul that the process was responsive to his and MetaEco's larger needs. Striking a balance between responsiveness and focus, MetaEco was able to close a deal with the news organization. If Tom hadn't exercised his new responsibility as Scrum-Master and hadn't protected the team's focus for the Sprint, things might have ended differently. Because Tom correctly applied Scrum rules, he was able to balance the needs of both the marketing and the development departments.

The Product Owner at MegaEnergy

The Product Owner's focus is return on investment (ROI). The Product Backlog provides the Product Owner with a powerful tool for directing the project, Sprint by Sprint, to provide the greatest value and ROI to the organization. The Product Owner uses the Product Backlog to give the highest priority to the requirements that are of highest value to the business, to insert nonfunctional requirements that lead to opportunistic releases and implementations of functionality, and to constantly adjust the product in response to changing business conditions, including new competitive offerings.

The Situation at MegaEnergy

MegaEnergy owns gas pipelines throughout North America and leases them to gas and oil producers. Everything about the company is large, from the length of its pipelines to the size of its projects. MegaEnergy's pipelines run through private property, and MegaEnergy has formal agreements with the property owners agreeing to pay them annual royalties. At the start of every calendar year, MegaEnergy sends out royalty checks. This might seem like a simple operation at first. But when you consider how frequently land ownership changes, you can see how complex an undertaking it really is.

To know where to send royalty checks, MegaEnergy had to know who owned each parcel of land. Its method of determining land ownership was archaic. About three months before the end of each year, MegaEnergy would print out a list of all the land that its pipelines traversed. These lists would be sent to various state and provincial government land registry departments. For a per-item fee, these departments would research and return to MegaEnergy the name and address of the current owner of each piece of land. MegaEnergy staff would check these names and addresses against the ones that it had recorded in its system and make any necessary changes. The entire process was extravagantly expensive and unnecessarily time-consuming. All communication with the various levels of government was on paper, and as a result, the MegaEnergy land department always looked like a paper factory.

The company had already undertaken two efforts to automate the process, and both had failed. These efforts were called the Title project. Because every state and province had different procedures, processes, and ways of communicating land ownership information, the MegaEnergy land department had trouble finding a common way to obtain and process information from the different government agencies. Compounding the problem, MegaEnergy managers had decided to couple the automation project with a project to remove the MegaEnergy land system data from the mainframes and reimplement it on less expensive servers.

The project had just been reconstituted for a third try when MegaEnergy decided to try using Scrum. Nothing else had worked, so what did MegaEnergy have to lose? Besides, it seemed as though Scrum would be the perfect development process for this project, given the great complexity of the situation. Ruth, a project manager from one of the previous attempts, was appointed ScrumMaster. Jane, the head of the MegaEnergy land department, was designated Product Owner.

The Product Owner in Action

Ruth and I helped Jane construct the Product Backlog. Because so much work had already been done during previous attempts, our task was relatively easy, although it soon became clear how important it was. Prioritizing the automation process over the move away from mainframes enabled us to get a grip on the project and give the team some work that it could actually accomplish.

Each Sprint produces business functionality that is potentially implementable. But because there is so much work to be done on product architecture and infrastructure during the first few Sprints, these Sprints deliver far less functionality than later Sprints. Accordingly, we minimized the amount of business functionality for the first Sprint. In the MegaEnergy project, Ruth and Jane decided that the team should try to automate only the title feed from the government agency that it knew best: the provincial government of Alberta.

Jane presented the Product Backlog at the Sprint planning meeting. As she and the team looked it over, they saw an opportunity. The MegaEnergy land database contained all titles on which royalties were owned. A data feed could be obtained from Alberta that contained only ownership changes over the last 12 months. Transactions could then be constructed for every hit between the feed and the land database. A land analyst in the MegaEnergy land department would reconcile these and update the MegaEnergy land database only when appropriate. The analyst would no longer need to check the name and address of every single title. By automating the feed, providing reconciliation screens, and reversing the process, the volume of work could be significantly reduced and automated at the same time. The team was pleased with this discovery. Now it could reformulate the land database to support the new requirements, learn and test new server technologies, and construct a generalized XML data stream that the land department might be able to use in interactions with every government agency.

Thirty days later, at the first Sprint review meeting, the team presented the product increment that it had produced during the Sprint. Jane had worked with the team throughout this period and already knew what would be presented, but she was delighted nonetheless. She asked me to explain what I'd meant when I said that the functionality demonstrated at the Sprint review meeting must be potentially ready for implementation. I told her that at the subsequent Sprint planning meeting, she could ask for this increment to be implemented during the next Sprint. Jane chose to do so and conducted a two-week implementation Sprint. Because most MegaEnergy pipelines originated in and were fed through Alberta, the functionality produced during this Sprint immediately reduced the land department's workload by more than 40 percent.

The Product Owner's Value

The Product Owner is responsible for the ROI of the project, which usually means that the Product Owner chooses to develop product functionality that solves critical business problems. Jane was able to fulfill this responsibility by sorting priorities in the Product Backlog to reflect requirements with the highest business value. She was also able to call for releases of functionality when the business benefit more than offset the costs of implementation. While Jane was watching the demonstration during the Sprint review, she realized how much this single increment of functionality could do for her department. She had checked with the team and confirmed that implementing this one increment immediately wouldn't cause any complications down the line.

Traditionally, customers get to state the requirements that optimize their ROI at the start of the project, but they don't get to assess the accuracy of their predictions until the project is completed. Scrum lets the Product Owner adjust the ROI much more frequently. Jane was able to realize business value within 45 days, even though she had failed to realize any value during the previous two failed attempts at automation. MegaEnergy realized ROI almost immediately on this project. Also, through Jane's wise selection of an implementation, Mega-Energy was able to see how rapidly automation can bring business benefits.

The Team at Service1st

In a huge reversal of ordinary management practices, Scrum makes the team responsible for managing development activities. Traditionally, the project manager tells the team what to do and manages its work. In Scrum, however, the team selects the work that it will do during each Sprint. After that initial selection is made, it is up to the team to figure out how to do the work at hand. The team decides how to turn the selected requirements into an increment of potentially shippable product functionality. The team devises its own tasks and figures out who will do them.

The pressure inherent in a 30-day Sprint, the commitment the team members make to each other to accomplish something, and the principles of self-organization and cross-functional responsibilities all help the team successfully fulfill this responsibility. The team unfailingly rises to the occasion and manages itself. When anyone outside the team tries to tell the team what to do, more damage than good usually results. I don't know why Scrum's self-organization works so well, but that hardly matters. After all, I know of hundreds of successful Scrum projects encompassing thousands of successful Sprints.

The Situation at Service1st

Service1st is a medium-size vendor of customer service software with a large number of domestic and international customers. Service1st's products are well-regarded in the industry, with a solid release at least once a year. The company's managers had decided that they wanted some developers to begin working on the next release of the company's software while the rest of the developers wrapped up the current release. A team was formed of people with the appropriate skills who weren't needed for the current release. Seventeen people, including engineering and testing leads, were on this team. At first, the managers used PERT and Gantt charts to direct the team's efforts. But the company had decided that it would be switching all of its development over to Scrum, and so this team made the change as well.

The Team in Action

I conducted a Quickstart exercise with the team. This intensive two-day session teaches the team members Scrum practices and gets the team's first Sprint underway. The training part of Quickstart went well. But when I got to the first part of the Sprint planning meeting, things started to disintegrate. The room was overcrowded: 17 team members were huddled around a small conference table, and interested parties formed a ring behind them. The room was so crowded that the more aggressive team members questioned and collaborated with the Product Owner while the more passive team members withdrew from the process. By the time I had moved on to the second part of the Sprint planning meeting, in which the team defines its Sprint Backlog, only the more aggressive team members were involved. I interrupted the more active participants several times to call on some of the quieter team members. I asked them what they would be working on. I made sure they knew that nothing feels worse than getting up in a Daily Scrum and saying that you haven't been doing anything and that you're not really involved with the project. Although my intentions were good, I only ended up making the quieter members of the team feel worse when I made this observation.

The team was simply too large. Optimally, a team should include seven people. During the Sprint planning meeting of a team of seven people, the team members lean forward, interact, collaborate, look each other in the eye, and form a plan of action. The 17-person team had found a way to do this by excluding the 10 less active members. Seven people were planning the Sprint, but the other 10 were sitting out the process. What could I do? I felt it was too late to reconstitute the team, so I decided to let things proceed—I would see what happened.

Several days later, I was attending this team's Daily Scrum. Much to my surprise, everyone was reporting about work accomplished and work planned. Of course, the Daily Scrum took 20 minutes with that many people, but it was an active, lively session, and the team members all seemed to be engaged in their work. I asked the team members to meet with me after the Daily Scrum. At that point, they explained that they had decided the managers had been mistaken when it created such a large team. They didn't want to confront their managers on the issue, figuring that, in its wisdom, the management team had a reason for assigning such a large number to the development team. But the original team simply wasn't functioning, and the Sprint wasn't getting under way. So the team decided to break itself into four subteams, each with three to five members. The engineering and testing leads helped formulate these subteams and divided the work to minimize coupling and maximize cohesion. These leads took responsibility for resolving any dependencies among team members as work progressed. The leads were part of the team that committed to the work, so their actions were part of the self-organization.

I've believed in the power of a self-organizing team, but this team was especially impressive. It had organized itself into an optimum grouping of team members and found a way to resolve its dependencies. If a third party had tried to devise such a complicated scheme, it would have taken days and been very difficult to explain to all of the parties involved. But when the team tackled the problem collectively, it was able to cut up the problem quickly into manageable chunks.

The Team's Value

A team member pulled me aside later and told me that the key to the team's successful reorganization was my discussion about management responsibilities. I had told them that the team was responsible for managing itself and had full authority to do anything to meet the Sprint goal within the guidelines, standards, and conventions of the organization and of Scrum. The team had fully committed to the Sprint goal, and it had simply tried to figure out how it could meet that goal. No one had told the team that it wasn't allowed to reorganize, so it went ahead and did so.

Conclusions

At MetaEco, Tom protected the team's productivity and ability to meet its commitments by fulfilling his job as ScrumMaster. At MetaEnergy, Jane optimized the value of the development project by performing her duties as Product Owner. At Service1st, the Team fulfilled its responsibility of managing itself to meet its commitments by forming subteams.

In each of these instances, the action of each manager was very important to the success of the project. All of these actions required intelligence and initiative. However, each was a natural response to project events made visible by Scrum. Tom saw the deleterious effects of Paul's predations at the Daily Scrum when team members reported that he had redirected their work. Jane saw the opportunity of the early release at the Sprint review meeting. The Service1st team saw that it had to do something to get under way once the Sprint started. Scrum is structured to regularly make the state of the project visible to the three managers—the Product Owner, the ScrumMaster, and the Team—so that they can rapidly adjust the project to best meet its goals.

3

The ScrumMaster

Why did I choose a strange name like "ScrumMaster" for the person who facilitates Scrum projects? Why didn't I continue to use the standard title "project manager"? I wanted to highlight the extent to which the responsibilities of the ScrumMaster are different from those of a traditional project manager. This difference in terminology is symbolic of a drastic change managers must make to their approach if they are to effectively manage Scrum projects.

The authority of the ScrumMaster is largely indirect; it springs mainly from the ScrumMaster's knowledge of Scrum rules and practices and his or her work to ensure that they are followed. The ScrumMaster is responsible for the success of the project, and he or she helps increase the probability of success by helping the Product Owner select the most valuable Product Backlog and by helping the Team turn that backlog into functionality. The ScrumMaster earns no awards or medals because the ScrumMaster is only a facilitator.

Learning basic ScrumMaster practices is easy for most, but some people have difficulty learning the art of being a ScrumMaster. I've encountered some misguided Scrum implementations that don't have as much of an impact as they might have had because the ScrumMaster doesn't understand the philosophy underlying the Scrum methodology. Some ScrumMasters just don't get it, no matter how much they've read about Scrum. Scrum is a simple, straightforward set of practices, rules, and roles, as introduced in Chapter 1 and further described in the Appendixes of this book. But the philosophy behind Scrum is somewhat less simple and can sometimes be difficult to understand. Learning Scrum is a little like learning to ride a bike: after a little bit of time, you just get it—and your muscles get it—and from then on, it's as easy as pie. But until then, you'd better not go riding on major roads. ScrumMasters who don't fully understand Scrum are like novice bicyclists riding down major highways.

As Scrum spreads, I've become more concerned about ensuring that there is an adequate supply of qualified ScrumMasters. I recently received a call from a manager of a production team developing semiconductors for a large company in Texas. He wanted to know about "this Scrum stuff." I asked him what had piqued his interest, and he responded that four months earlier the manager of the design team in Germany had called and said to him, "We've adopted Scrum to manage our design process, so don't expect the usual reports." Yesterday, the same individual had called to tell the Texas manager that the design team had slipped and was three weeks behind schedule. The Texas manager wanted to know, "Is this Scrum?"

This kind of call is all too familiar to me. In another instance, a manager from Brazil came up to me after a class at a recent conference. He was quite excited about the idea of Daily Scrums. He told me he had been using Scrum for more than six months, and he thought implementing a Daily Scrum would really help communications within the team. I couldn't believe that he had read about Scrum but not understood how critical the Daily Scrum is for socialization and synchronization.

These examples show how easy it is for people to misunderstand Scrum. People tend to interpret Scrum within the context of their current project management methodologies. They apply Scrum rules and practices without fully understanding the underlying principles of self-organization, emergence, and visibility and the inspection/adaptation cycle. They don't understand that Scrum involves a paradigm shift from control to empowerment, from contracts to collaboration, and from documentation to code.

Let's look at the experiences of ScrumMasters with differing levels of experience with Scrum. These examples should help us understand how important it is to have a well-qualified ScrumMaster herding the team.

The Untrained ScrumMaster at Trey Research

A consultant is sometimes defined as someone who gives advice more than 100 miles from where he or she lives. I know why this is the case. My neighbors know my lawn has patches and crabgrass in it, just as their lawns do. The police in my town know I sometimes speed. The librarians know I sometimes have overdue books, and they know I have a taste for daring mystery stories. In short, the other residents of my town know I am a regular person with both strengths and shortcomings—I'm not at every moment an expert on all questions.

People often hire consultants because they want to get a different perspective on their situations. This new perspective is often perceived as somehow better than the native view of things. This would be enough of a reason for clients to think twice before hiring a local consultant. So you can imagine how excited I was when a company in the town where my family has lived for the last 23 years called. The CIO had implemented Scrum and wanted me to check it out.

The company in question was Trey Research, a start-up company that acquires tissue cultures from healthcare organizations and resells them to pharmaceutical companies. Trey Research adds value to the cultures by inventorying and identifying the demographics, illness, and stage of illness represented by each sample. Overloaded with new systems to build and implement, the Trey Research CIO had implemented Scrum. He wanted me to evaluate how Scrum was working at his company and suggest how his implementation might be improved.

What Was Wrong

At the beginning of my visit, I met with the CIO's management team and provided them with an overview of Scrum. We then discussed the various projects under way at Trey Research and how they were using Scrum. Each team had sprinted several times, and everyone was pleased with the changes that had been effected and the progress that had been made.

The ScrumMaster who had been using Scrum the most invited me to attend "his Daily Scrum." The moment I heard this, an alarm bell went off in my head. Why was it "his Daily Scrum" and not "the team's Daily Scrum"? I decided to hold my tongue and wait to find out. He led me to a large room in the basement of the old mansion that was Trey Research headquarters. Nine developers were working at their workstations—five clustered in the center of the room and a pair at each end of the room. From a structural point of view, this was good news: an open work area like this enables the high-bandwidth communication essential for successful teamwork.

At this meeting, the ScrumMaster kicked things off by pulling out a list. Reading from the list, he proceeded to go around the room, asking each person present whether he or she had completed the tasks he had written by that person's name. He asked questions like, "Mary, did you finish designing the screen I gave you yesterday? Are you ready to start on the dialog boxes in it today?" Once he had exhausted his list and spoken to everyone in the room, he asked whether the team needed any help from him. The team members were all silent.

I wasn't sure how to tell him what I thought of his methods. On one hand, work in my hometown was certainly convenient. But how could he have so completely misunderstood all that I had written about Scrum? How had I failed to convey the spirit of Scrum? He turned to me and somewhat proudly asked what I thought. I paused and then complimented him on the open arrangement of the team room and the general spirit of the team. I then asked him how he knew what the team was working on. He started to say he knew because they were working on what he had told them to work on, but before the entire sentence got out, a look of shock passed over his face. In just a moment of reflection, he had identified the key element of Scrum that he had forgotten to implement.

Lessons Learned

The project manager had read the book on Scrum and learned the mechanics of the Daily Scrum. He had read that team members are supposed to answer three questions at each Daily Scrum:

- What have I done since the last Daily Scrum?

- What am I going to do between now and the next Daily Scrum?

- What is preventing me from doing my work?

However, he was a longtime practitioner of traditional project management techniques. He'd spent years planning tasks and ensuring that teams completed them. Consequently, he had interpreted what he'd read as

- He would check on whether the team members had done what he told them to do since the last Daily Scrum.

- He would tell each member what they should do between now and the next Daily Scrum.

- He would check to see whether he could do anything to help the team accomplish its goals.

To save time, he had shortened the last question into a general inquiry.

The shift from project manager to ScrumMaster had eluded him. He believed that Scrum was merely a series of practices and techniques for implementing iterative, incremental development. He missed the subtle but critical shift from controlling to facilitating, from bossing to coaching. Just as he missed out on these changes, he also missed out on the importance of a self-organizing team. He and the team had committed to a Sprint goal, but the team never self-organized or truly committed to the Scrum goal. The productivity that emerges when a team figures out the best way to accomplish its goals hadn't been realized. Neither did team members have the deep personal commitment that emerges when people puzzle their way through their work on their own. The team's ability to tackle its problems and solve them is the heart of Scrum and the basis of the Scrum team's extraordinary productivity. Once I pointed this out to the project manager, he immediately saw the error of his ways. "Oh, of course!" he exclaimed. Some people are so embedded in their familiar ways that they have trouble seeing what they have to change, no matter how many articles and books they read and agree with.

The Untrained ScrumMaster at Litware

Litware is a medium-size vendor of planning software. A project management office consisting of one manager, John Chen, and three project managers planned all of the company's releases. After each release was planned, the work was broken down into tasks and organized on PERT charts. These tasks were then divided among the various analysts, designers, programmers, testers, and documenters. The approach was very "waterfall" and very defined. As the complexity of the releases increased and the customer base grew, the release planning phase grew and grew until it was simply unacceptable. The results of each release planning phase were also unsatisfactory: the plans were difficult to adapt to the complexities that the team encountered and to the changes that sales and customers requested.

The company's frustrated managers asked John to work with me to switch the release management over to Scrum. After assessing the situation, John and I set a Scrum start date several weeks out. At this point, we would convert the plans to Product Backlog, provide Scrum training, and then conduct several Sprint planning meetings.

What Was Wrong

During those several weeks, I held a Certified ScrumMaster class and invited John to attend. This was his chance to learn Scrum before he implemented it at Litware. The class prepares people who will be ScrumMasters for projects. As usual, the class was well attended. Unfortunately, there was one conspicuous no-show: John. I kept checking during the day, but he was definitely not there. Later that day, I e-mailed John to find out what had happened. John responded that other priorities at work had precluded his attendance but that we would nonetheless start the Scrum implementation as we'd planned.

I showed up on the appointed day, and we spent the morning laying out the Product Backlog for two teams. In the afternoon, the Litware managers asked me to give an overview of Scrum to the entire development organization. The managers wanted everyone to understand Scrum and what was planned for the two teams. I introduced Scrum and entertained many questions. Everyone wanted to know where Scrum had been used before, how it worked, and what everyone's new roles would be. They were particularly intrigued by the concept of self-organization because they weren't big fans of task-driven work assigned to them by a project manager. I spent quite a bit of time discussing the shift from project manager to ScrumMaster. I compared the ScrumMaster to a sheepdog who would do anything to protect its flock, or team. We discussed how the team's welfare was the ScrumMaster's highest responsibility and how the ScrumMaster would do anything in his or her power to help the team be productive. At the end of the training session, John and I confirmed the start time with the teams that we were beginning to work with the next day.

I was setting up for the Sprint planning meeting the next morning when Elsa Leavitt, a member of John's staff, arrived to let me know that John had called her and said he would be at an offsite meeting instead of at the Sprint planning meeting. He had sent Elsa along in his stead. John hadn't gotten it: a sheepdog never gets distracted from the flock. John didn't understand that the team would be relying on him. Worse, he had sent a message that Scrum and the team were unimportant to him. He had indicated that he valued offsite meetings more than building software—even though it was the software that was critical to the success of Litware.

I filled in the vice president of development on the situation. He understood the significance of John's absence. He immediately promoted Elsa and appointed her to be the team's ScrumMaster. When the team members arrived for the Sprint planning session, they found that Elsa was their ScrumMaster. She took care of them just as a good sheepdog would.

Lessons Learned

John didn't understand that ScrumMasters have to make a personal commitment to their teams. A ScrumMaster would no more delegate his responsibilities than a sheepdog would lie down for a nap while herding the flock. The team needs to sense that someone is deeply invested in its work and will protect and help it no matter what. The ScrumMaster's attitude should reflect the importance of the project; instead, John's attitude told the team that things at Litware were still business as usual.

I believe that John didn't want to understand the role of ScrumMaster. The behavior of the ScrumMaster is dramatically different from that of people staffing a formal project management office that assigns work and controls its completion. The shift from having authority to being a facilitator was too much for John. Not only is the ScrumMaster role one without authority, but it also potentially represented a career change that John didn't want to make. The ScrumMaster is a leader, not a manager. The ScrumMaster earns the team's respect because he or she fulfills the duties of the role and not simply because he or she was assigned the role in the first place.

The shift from delegating to being personally responsible is difficult for some people to accept. The "hands-on" aspect of Scrum scares some people. John deselected himself from Scrum by failing to show up for the job. The vice president of development made the right move by reassigning the role of ScrumMaster to someone who recognized its importance.

Overzealous at Contoso.com

Contoso is a software vendor that provides administrative, clinical, and radiology software to healthcare providers. In the late 1990s, a number of dot-com companies were funded to initiate Web-based alternatives to Contoso's products. These new competitors intended to encroach on Contoso by initially offering patient-to-physician portals. These portals would facilitate patient and physician healthcare interactions, including prescription services, healthcare queries, appointments, and online medical advisories. Contoso viewed the portals as Trojan horses through which these competitors would later start offering administrative and billing services as Application Service Providers to Contoso's customers.

To counter this threat, Contoso formed a dot-com subsidiary, Contoso.com. This subsidiary would offer its own patient-to-physician portal, with the difference that its portal would be linked to existing Contoso systems. Several projects were quickly initiated, including development projects, marketing projects, and a public relations project. I was the ScrumMaster for several of these projects, including the public relations project. The public relations project's goal was to increase the marketplace's awareness of Contoso's new strategy and to get current and potential customers to see Contoso.com as an alternative to the other new dot-coms.

Being Right Isn't Everything

The public relations project was very aggressive. In its first Sprint, a public relations firm was hired and a public relations plan conceived and approved. In its second Sprint, Contoso.com and the public relations firm began executing the plan, a key element of which was to make various analyst firms aware that Contoso.com was alive in the Internet space and was a purveyor of Web services. Several analysts had issued reports on this space and not mentioned Contoso in any of them. Many of Contoso's customers were interested in these services but weren't aware that their own vendor was a potential provider.

After considerable effort, the public relations firm was able to set up an all-day session with Contoso.com management and some key analysts. We were to present our plan, our offerings, and our timetable. Our hope was that by the end of the day, these analysts thought of Contoso when they thought of Internet healthcare and healthcare portals.

At the Daily Scrum the day prior to the analyst meeting, one of the team members reported an impediment. I could tell it was going to be a big one from the looks on the faces of all the team members. The vice president in charge of Contoso.com had called for a mandatory offsite meeting the next day. All hands were to be on deck, and all prior commitments were to be canceled. I was incredulous. What could be more important than our Sprint goal, to get Contoso.com visible as a viable alternative to the other dot-coms? The team told me what was more important: the vice president was concerned about morale at Contoso.com and was holding a picnic to improve everyone's mood.

I knew that this was a mistake. The offsite was an impediment to the Sprint. Ironically, it was more likely to hurt team morale than help it. I was certain that the vice president was unaware of the analyst meeting. Otherwise, why would she have insisted on everyone's attendance? To my everlasting amazement, it turned out that she was well aware of the analyst meeting. She even went so far as to ask me to call the analysts and cancel it. She required complete participation at the offsite out of concern that allowing anyone to be absent would encourage everyone to skip out. Unfortunately, I got pretty heated as I was expressing my opinion of this policy. She refused to let the analyst meeting proceed and showed me out of her office.

I was seeing red. I was the sheepdog, and a wolf had attacked the flock. I quickly escalated this impediment to the senior managers. I was sure that they would see the fallacy of the decision and advise the vice president to reconsider. I hadn't anticipated that they would view teamwork as more important than progress and that they would see the sheepdog as an impediment. I was let go shortly thereafter.

Lessons Learned

The ScrumMaster's job is to protect the team from impediments during the Sprint. However, the ScrumMaster has to operate within the culture of the organization. My mistake lay in failing to recognize the value of teamwork to this organization. I had been a consultant for so long that I'd forgotten how much some large organizations cared about not rocking the boat and keeping the corporate family together.

The ScrumMaster walks a fine line between the organization's need to make changes as quickly as possible and its limited tolerance for change.

Whenever possible, the ScrumMaster makes a case and pushes the necessary changes through. The results are often greater productivity and greater return on investment (ROI). However, sometimes these changes are culturally unacceptable and the ScrumMaster must acquiesce. Remember that Scrum is the art of the possible. A dead sheepdog is a useless sheepdog.

Wolves at MegaFund

MegaFund is one of the largest fund management companies in the world. Its innovative funds attracted investors more than the funds at any other organization. However, by 1997, Charles Schwab, eTrade, and other financial companies had revolutionized stock trading. Customers could now manage their own fund accounts, buy and sell stocks, and play the margins without personal assistance from professional stock brokers. The Internet and mobile technology had enabled Web, PDA, cell-phone, and voice-response unit functionality. Unfortunately, MegaFund had fallen behind this revolution. Its technology organization was large, bureaucratic, and cumbersome. To make matters worse, it had implemented Capability Maturity Model Level 3 practices over the last year. If incorrectly implemented, these practices can increase bureaucracy, as they had at MegaFund. MegaFund was now so bureaucratic that it was hard to get anything done.

MegaFund explored ways to enable new technologies that could access the legacy databases where all customer account and trade information was stored. After several false starts, MegaFund managers decided to do it the right way. Usually when managers say that they're going to do a project "the right way," that project ends up dying from excess overhead. Sure enough, after nine months the project was stalled while battles raged over what sort of technology to use. Should it be Solaris, Microsoft Windows NT 4.0, or AIX? Should Mega-Fund standardize on Intel technology? Were Sun servers more scalable than IBM servers? Was COM the way of the future, or was CORBA the way to go? While these wars were being waged, the competition surged ahead.

MegaFund finally decided to bring in Scrum to break the logjam and get the project moving. Terry Adams, who had been the project manager, had a strong technical background and an intuitive understanding of his new role as ScrumMaster. During the Daily Scrum, he listened carefully to each team member's report. When someone had a problem with his or her equipment, Terry lent a hand. When people were stuck, Terry helped them access expertise external to the project. When purchase orders didn't go through, Terry helped expedite them. He was able to remove impediments without ruffling feathers and without endangering his job.

The Wolves Strike

The team started a Sprint, and within two weeks it had made an impressive amount of progress. The team had selected and begun to use its tools and was implementing the first transactions. By the end of the Sprint, the team would demonstrate an approach to solving MegaFund's technology problems and implementing a suite of competitive solutions.

Russell Hunter, a senior vice president in MegaFund's systems company, was at a cocktail party about this time. After months of trouble, Russ was finally able to brag about some progress. Russ boasted to the head of the electronic funds retail unit, who commented that he had some significant competitive problems that he would like to see solved by this team. Russ, spotting an opportunity to garner some good will, offered to demonstrate a key electronic funds retail transaction at the Sprint review. The next morning, Russ got to the office early and approached one of the systems engineers on the team. The engineer didn't report to Russ. He reported to someone who reported to someone who reported to Russ. Russ was a legend to him, someone who could influence his career with as little as a sidelong glance. When Russ asked him to look into implementing this transaction as part of the Sprint, the engineer couldn't say no.

Something strange happened during that day's Daily Scrum. Terry was listening carefully as usual, so he immediately noticed that this particular engineer reported progress in work that wasn't part of the Sprint goal or selected Product Backlog. Terry asked the engineer to meet with him after the Daily Scrum, at which point the engineer confessed that he'd been asked to do a favor. The engineer was accustomed to senior managers telling him to do something on the side. But Terry knew that this practice was a violation of a fundamental Scrum rule: the team is left alone during the Sprint to accomplish the goals to which it initially committed.

Terry was an intuitive ScrumMaster. He went to Russ and asked about the work that Russ had asked the engineer to do for him. Russ was immediately defensive, knowing that he had violated one of the rules of Scrum. Russ said that it was as though he'd seen a $20 bill on the ground and he couldn't help but pick it up. Instead of criticizing Russ, Terry struck a sympathetic posture. He made it clear to Russ that he understood the importance of this opportunity. However, he said, since Scrum was new to MegaFund, he was sure that Russ was unaware that Scrum had mechanisms for dealing with opportunities like this one. In a case like this, whenever an opportunity arose that was more important than the work selected by the team for the Sprint, management could abnormally terminate the Sprint. The Team, the Product Owner, and management would then conduct a new Sprint planning meeting. The new opportunity would be selected if it truly was the top-priority Product Backlog.

Russ thought about it for several seconds and realized that he didn't want to cancel the Sprint. Everyone would know that he was responsible for halting progress on the project for this minor opportunity. The Sprint planning meeting would make his act highly visible and provide his peers with an opportunity to ask why his pet project was more important than their needs. Russ thanked Terry but demurred, saying that he would meet with the Product Owner and get on the Product Backlog in the next Sprint planning session. Of course, he never did so.

Lessons Learned

Terry used the Scrum rules and practices to keep the project on track. Scrum offers many opportunities to make changes and to respond to new opportunities. Scrum also keeps everything highly visible. The Product Backlog and its prioritization are open to everyone so that they can discuss them and come to the best way to optimize ROI. The Daily Scrum keeps all team activities visible so that the ScrumMaster can enforce the rules and help the team stay on track. By keeping everything in full view, the type of backroom politicking and influence swapping normal in most organizations is minimized. These mechanisms are useful in bureaucratic organizations as a way to get particular things done. But when Scrum is already getting things done, these behind-the-scenes pressures are counterproductive.

Conclusions

At Trey Research and Litware, we saw that it's not always easy to understand the role of the ScrumMaster. At Contoso.com, we saw how a ScrumMaster can self-destruct. At MegaFund, we saw a ScrumMaster both fulfill his responsibilities and embed Scrum practices and rules in the organization. Something unique happened in each situation. The ScrumMaster was aware of Scrum's practices and rules and responded. Sometimes the response was good for the organization, and sometimes it wasn't good. In each instance, the ScrumMaster interpreted the job differently, and the results varied dramatically.

Over the last several years, I've wrestled with the question of how to make the difference between project manager and ScrumMaster, between coach and boss, more readily understood. How can I explain the shift in a way that is easy to absorb regardless of a person's background and inclination? When experienced Scrum practitioners are around to mentor a new ScrumMaster, the transition to Scrum is usually smooth. When I mentor new ScrumMasters, for example, I can help them understand many of the consequences of failure in part because I've failed so many times! I can also show them the difference between failure and success. We first fill the role of ScrumMaster ourselves, setting an example. Then we invite the new ScrumMaster to begin. We coach the new ScrumMaster after every meeting and throughout the day. We point out opportunities for the ScrumMaster to help the team. We point out ways that the ScrumMaster can tell when the team needs help. We also point out instances in which the ScrumMaster is controlling rather than guiding and explain what the consequences of such acts are likely to be.

The ScrumMaster is responsible for making sure that all the pieces of the Scrum process come together and work as a whole. The Product Owner must do his or her job. The Team must do its job. The chickens must be kept in line. The Product Owner and the Team must collaborate appropriately and use the Scrum meetings for inspection and adaptation.

The responsibilities of the ScrumMasters can be summarized as follows:

- Remove the barriers between development and the Product Owner so that the Product Owner directly drives development.

- Teach the Product Owner how to maximize ROI and meet his or her objectives through Scrum.

- Improve the lives of the development team by facilitating creativity and empowerment.

- Improve the productivity of the development team in any way possible.

- Improve the engineering practices and tools so that each increment of functionality is potentially shippable.

- Keep information about the team's progress up-to-date and visible to all parties.

When the ScrumMaster fulfills these responsibilities, the project usually stays on track. These responsibilities should be enough to keep the ScrumMaster busy; no ScrumMaster should have any time left over to act like a typical boss. Indeed, a ScrumMaster who acts like a program manager probably isn't fulfilling all of his or her duties as a ScrumMaster.

In my experience, some people intuitively understand the ScrumMaster role and take to it like a duck to water. Others struggle to understand Scrum and sometimes make harmful mistakes as they learn. However, even the successful ScrumMaster requires several Sprints to get going. When I am unclear about how to help a Scrum project, I've found it useful to keep the homily "the art of the possible" in mind. Focus on what can be done rather than be frustrated by what can't be done. This thought helps guide my actions at work on projects and in everyday life.

4

Bringing Order from Chaos

In software development organizations, chaos often results when a project's complexity is greater than its managers' ability to direct meaningful progress toward a goal. Progress might be made in fits and starts, but it is often indiscernible and unsatisfactory. Scrum cuts through this kind of complexity and wrests order from chaos. It does so by enabling a team to organize itself, which allows a particularly productive order to emerge. Let's visit several organizations to look at them before Scrum, to see how Scrum brought order to their projects, and to then generalize some practices from the experiences of these organizations. In these examples, we'll see the power of *time-boxing* to instill the art of the possible and avoid the pursuit of perfection, the practice of *incremental delivery* to improve engineering practices, and the practice of *empowerment* and *self-organization* to foster creativity and worker satisfaction.

The first organization we'll consider is Service1st, an independent software vendor of customer service applications that was introduced in Chapter 2. Service1st traditionally planned and managed its complex projects using extensive PERT charts. The results were less than stellar: the home stretch of every project was impressively chaotic and was invariably followed by an extended period of employee exhaustion and apathy. The second organization we'll look at is Tree Business Publishing. Tree's push to move its trade journals onto the Web coincided with several other big and messy initiatives, nearly paralyzing the development groups and causing extensive schedule slippage. The third organization is Lapsec, a research and development organization that builds proof of concept applications for the U.S. government. In the wake of September 11, Lapsec was called on to rapidly develop new information concerning potential terrorist activities. This project required melding a number of technologies and an untested capability called *data fusion*, an advanced agent-based form of data mining.

The Situation at Service1st

Service1st's development organization typically generated a new release of its software at least every year. The last two months of each development cycle were always a fire drill, and the result of each push for a new release was always an exhausted staff and buggy software. The company's managers had resolved to even out the intensity of the development effort over the six-month cycle, thereby relieving the development organization and improving the quality of each release.

Upon my arrival, the vice president of development took me on a tour of the engineering space. It was absolutely empty and completely still: perhaps one in four offices or cubicles was occupied. At first, I thought that it was so early in the morning that nobody had arrived yet. When I realized that it was already 9 o'clock, I considered that maybe a recent layoff had decimated the ranks. But no—Service1st was a growing and successful software company and hadn't had any layoffs since it was founded more than 20 years ago.

The vice president explained the situation to me: the company had just finished a six-month development cycle, the last release had gone out three weeks ago, and the staff was still totally exhausted. Developers had spent the last two months working evenings and weekends to complete the release in time. Not only was this bad for Service1st's employees, but it was also bad for its customers: because of the frantic pace of the last leg of each release's development, bugs often crept into the software and went unnoticed. The vice president said that he wanted to implement Scrum because he never wanted to put such demands on his staff again and because he wanted to improve the quality of Service1st's software.

What was the method behind this madness? How had the development staff gotten so overwhelmed? At the beginning of every development release, program managers coordinated with marketing to create detailed work plans for developing new functionality. The functionality list was derived from customer enhancement requests, high-priority bug fixes, performance enhancements, and competitive features. After a plan was established, modifications to the plan were handled through a formal change control process.

The work plans were represented in PERT and Gantt charts, with detailed resource leveling. The work was divided into numerous feature sets with high cohesion and low coupling, maximizing the proximity of work and reducing the dependencies. Anyone working on one feature set was unlikely to interact with someone working on another feature set. The only people for whom this isolated condition was not the case were those lucky souls assigned to work on multiple teams. Members of the development staff were given assignments and instructed to work on them until the release had been completed.

Complicating matters considerably, the development staff was assigned tasks by role; roles included analysis, design, coding, testing, and documentation. This method resulted in a waterfall way of thinking about work. One individual would analyze the requirement, another person would design the requirement, the next person would code the design, and then, finally, someone else would test the code. Rather than working together as a team, developers worked as though they were individuals at an assembly plant, passing the product along the line once they'd made their respective contributions. This method provided no opportunities for collaboration. Furthermore, the sequential nature of the work caused work to start and stop over and over again as people waited for one another to complete antecedent tasks.

Everyone in the development group had a lot to accomplish, so why wasn't the whole department hard at work at 9 A.M.? The vice president observed that the team usually didn't feel any pressure until three months before the release date and that members of the team started developing in earnest only during the last two months of the release cycle. Assignments at the task level, assignment of individuals to multiple teams, and particularly the waterfall approach all led everyone to feel isolated from the reality of the release during the first three or four months. During the last two months, the developers tried to make up for what they hadn't completed in the first four months.

The next release was due April 7 and was to be demonstrated at a user conference in March. Now was only the end of October. The staff was focusing on the upcoming holidays while recovering from the crunch of the last release cycle. Meanwhile, although it was only three weeks into the new release cycle, managers' anxiety levels were already high. Would the release be on time? Would the staff have to work like dogs again for the last two months? Nothing seemed to have changed, so everyone was expecting the worst.

Application of Scrum

Service1st's managers asked me to help them introduce Scrum as its development process. The company wanted all of the development organization transitioned to Scrum within two weeks. I started with the team that was working on a complicated piece of code to be incorporated into the next release: workflow capabilities.

Service1st had partnered with another software company and licensed its workflow products. During the development of this release, one team from each organization would work together to determine how the products would interact and figure out how to implement some workflow functionality. Members of the workflow team had been assigned tasks intended to further the design of four workflows. The folks in program management had selected these four workflows because together they represented a cohesive transaction.

The vice president thought that Scrum might be particularly effective with the workflow team because it was dealing with so many unknowns. He had scheduled a time for me to meet with the team so that I could get a feel for what they were doing and what progress they'd made thus far. I thought this would be a good opportunity to help the team understand a bit about Scrum; to that end, I conducted the meeting as a Daily Scrum.

The team members described their situation to me. Some of them told me that they were investigating how the two products could work together. The interaction between the products was intricate and complex. The team was struggling to determine how a single login could be used. Some were concerned that the security and authority schemes of the two products might be misaligned because each product had security mechanisms that were invoked based on user authority established at login. The team reported that although it had been working on this problem for three weeks, it could make only limited progress because the people who'd been assigned analysis work were still trying to determine how the products would be integrated in the first place. The people doing analysis were stuck, and so the other members of the team were sitting and twiddling their thumbs. They were spending their days redesigning their screens and databases to match the latest results from the people doing integration analysis.

I came away from this Daily Scrum meeting with the impression that this team didn't own its work. Someone had told the team what to do, and it was dutifully following instructions. I decided that a Sprint planning meeting would help the team focus its efforts on a small set of pressing problems and allow it to achieve some concrete results. I determined that I would ask the team to make the two products work together just enough to support one transaction that used workflow functionality. I asked the team to set aside the next day for a Sprint planning meeting, explaining that during this meeting we would figure out whether over the course of a 30-day Sprint we could build something that demonstrated integration of the two products.

We began work the next day at 9 A.M. by listing tasks the team was working on. We then wrote down the requirements for the four workflows from which tasks had been derived. After some prompting, the team members decided that the top priority was credit initiation workflow. They pointed out that work on the other workflows couldn't begin until the credit initiation workflow was complete. I questioned them about nonfunctional requirements that had to be addressed to support the workflow. We came up with the following list of requirements, both functional and nonfunctional:

1. Credit initiation workflow login

2. Credit initiation workflow startup

3.   Consistent unified product appearance

4.   Consistent security through both products

5.   Seamless and scalable operation

I explained to the team the concept of the tracer bullet, introduced by Andy Hunt and Dave Thomas in *The Pragmatic Programmer* (Addison-Wesley, 1999). Someone firing a machine pistol in the dark is unable to aim it. But adding luminescence to every fiftieth bullet enables the person firing the gun to see a trail that can be used to adjust aim. I asked the team to build a tracer bullet of functionality through the system to demonstrate the path for all other functionality. Could the team build part or all of the login and credit initiation workflow operating through both products and meet all of the nonfunctional requirements identified in the Product Backlog prior to Workflow 2? And could the team complete this work in a 30-day Sprint?

The team members were intrigued and excited. All they had to do was develop a small piece of functionality that served both products in such a way that the customer could perceive only a single product. The team would be building demonstrable functionality in just a month. The team would have to design only a few screens to demonstrate this capability, so it wouldn't have to waste time designing and redesigning numerous screens and database tables. The team was going to accomplish something concrete within a short period of time. Team members could almost taste their own success. They wouldn't have to wait through the end of the release for a feeling of accomplishment.

Managers would benefit from this arrangement, too: they would learn early the degree to which the two products could interoperate. Using this knowledge, they then could revisit the question of what functionality to incorporate in this release. The first Sprint would remove uncertainty and permit managers to focus resources on areas of real possibility. The workflow integration team was helping managers make decisions based on certainties instead of hunches and speculations. By introducing iterative, incremental development driven by a single Product Backlog, Service1st could produce a solid foundation of functionality upon which it could base the rest of the release cycle.

Lessons Learned

We can see from the example of Service1st the difficulty of trying to figure out everything in advance in a complex project. The interaction of the two products was so complex and so unknown that the tasks managers had planned at the beginning of the release cycle were obsolete soon after they'd been assigned. Just a moment after the team began work, the project slipped. Planned tasks couldn't be completed and dependent tasks were put on hold indefinitely. Team members struggled to reconcile the work they needed to do with the work that had been assigned to them.

We can see that the sequential nature of the tasks divided the team. The people who analyzed the situation and set requirements were not the same people who would design the solutions that met these requirements. The people who designed these solutions were not the same people who would code the solutions. The team was fundamentally divided. How did this divided team manage to communicate and collaborate? Not very well: after each task had been completed, team members had to produce a document detailing the work they'd done.

We can also see that the team didn't feel that it was making progress toward release. But what other choice did this group have? Only when the last two months arrived and the urgency set in did management give up on its plan and allow the team to do what it needed to get the release built. But by then there wasn't enough time, so the team would have to work nights and weekends. The developers never had enough time both to build functionality and to debug it, so the releases were bug-ridden and customers wasn't as happy as they ought to have been.

By focusing on increments of functionality, the team makes orderly progress toward completing the release. Since each increment is tested as it is coded, the number of bugs never overwhelms the project. Scrum's iterative incremental practices provide the team with a sense of accomplishment and an awareness of where it is in the release cycle. Scrum's requirement that each increment of code be potentially shippable requires the incremental removal of defects and minimizes ongoing bugs.

Scrum is an empirical process. Rather than following outdated scripts, Scrum employs frequent inspection and adaptation to direct team activities toward a desired goal. The Sprint review inspection is particularly powerful because real functionality is being inspected. When they use Scrum, teams are empowered to find their own way through complex situations. This freedom, along with the creativity that results from it, is one of the core benefits of Scrum.

The Situation at Tree Business Publishing

Tree Business Publishing (Tree), a division of Tree Holdings, publishes professional journals across a diverse range of industries. It has been almost a decade since Tree decided to publish its journals not only in print but also on the Web. The editors in charge of Tree's trade publications were told to have journals on the Web as soon as possible. However, two years after this directive had been issued, only one journal was Web live. The delay was in part because Web publishing turned out not to be as similar to print publishing as everyone had thought. Progress had been stymied because Tree had yet to answer a series of questions specific to Web publishing:

- How could a journal be presented tastefully and effectively online?

- How would internal editorial and production processes change as journals began to publish online as well as in print?

- What was the best mechanism for getting content onto the Web?

Tree's editors, writers, and software development teams had spent some time trying to arrive at an acceptable solution. At first, all of the editors attempted to construct "media-neutral" publishing solutions. The publishing process would generate XML data streams that could be used to render content in any format the business wanted. Even though the managers at Tree had decided that this was the right thing to do, they had also decided that media-neutral content development and management was more challenging than they had first thought. The goal of moving over to a media-neutral mode of operation had added a level of complexity that stymied any progress toward the immediate goal of getting Tree's trade journals up on the Web.

In desperation, Tree's managers sought a way to speed up delivery of the journals to the Web. They lighted upon WebPub, a small two-year-old dot-com capable of quickly generating content-rich Web sites. WebPub already had a number of customers that had already successfully used its products to publish online. Tree bought WebPub and declared it to be the Web publishing solution for all of the Tree journals. These journals were to rethink their Web publishing efforts and center them on WebPub.

Unfortunately, Tree's purchase of WebPub made the Web publishing problem more complex than ever. WebPub's Web publishing platform required enhancements before it would be able to publish Tree journals. Although Tree thought it had purchased a generalized solution, WebPub's platform had peculiarities that were specific to its legacy customer base. Now Tree had to decide whether to upgrade the WebPub platform so that it would be able to publish Tree journals or to turn the WebPub platform into a generalized publishing platform that could handle all kinds of Web publishing.

The following decisions were made to stop the floundering and enable progress:

- The WebPub platform would be enhanced with generalized publishing in mind, but the first enhancements to be made would be those that enabled Tree journals to get online.

■   XML media-neutral feeds would be generated from each journal's editorial process to feed the WebPub platform. XML was already the primary input for this platform. A generalized XML data type definition would have to be constructed to handle the requirements of all of the journals.

■   The journals' respective Web developers would halt all journal-specific Web development, learn to use the WebPub platform, and work to integrate the editorial process with the XML feeds into the WebPub platform.

These decisions represented a critical breakthrough for Tree in large part because they reduced the number of options available to the journals, to Web-Pub, and to the Tree business unit. However, these decisions also had harmful side effects: managers now felt that they could impose new deadlines for the Web publication of the journals. These deadlines were imminent, in large part because the company had to justify its rather costly acquisition of WebPub.

The WebPub developers were dependent on the results of two incomplete and undefined projects. Everything they did was subject to change as the journals' XML feeds were formalized and the WebPub platform was enhanced. The developers were shooting at a moving target, and that target was not slowing down.

Application of Scrum

Tree hired me to introduce Scrum at WebPub. I had first presented Scrum to them several years before. Managers remembered the presentation and felt that Scrum offered a possible solution. They particularly liked its incremental delivery of functionality providing a tangible demonstration of progress. Everyone felt an urgent need to get the journals published online. Over 100 people were involved in the effort to do so, but no progress was being made.

The individual efforts to enhance the WebPub platform, to standardize XML, and to publish journals on the Web were all completely and inextricably intertwined. Fortunately, Scrum teams are cross-functional. A Scrum of Scrums is the usual mechanism that coordinates multiple teams working on a single project, much as the Daily Scrum is the mechanism that coordinates the work of multiple people on a single team. A Scrum of Scrums is a Daily Scrum consisting of one member from each team in a multi-team project. Before a project officially begins, the planners of the project parse the work among teams to minimize dependencies. Teams then work on parts of the project architecture that are orthogonal to each other. However, this coordination mechanism is effective only when there are minor couplings or dependencies that require resolution. The dependencies at Tree were so significant that a Scrum of Scrums wouldn't work.

To quickly develop increments of product functionality, I needed XML, WebPub, and journal functionality developed in parallel. The XML and WebPub aspects of the work were extensive and of an infrastructural nature. How could the effort in these areas be coordinated with the work of teams building journal functionality? How could the XML and WebPub teams satisfy the requirements of the journal teams while working in parallel to deliver their own functionality?

I decided that the best option was for the individuals on each effort to coordinate these dependencies. The dependencies were too complex to parse before work began, so the teams would have to self-organize to resolve the dependencies. I asked Tree to select the four journals that it wanted online first. Each team was staffed with developers. We then assigned someone from the XML team and someone from the WebPub team to each of these journal teams.

I held a Sprint planning meeting for each journal team. Each journal team had about nine members, including the part-time XML member and the part-time WebPub member. I worked with the first team and its journal editor, who was designated the Product Owner. We constructed a Product Backlog of functionality. We inserted into the top-priority Product Backlog those nonfunctional requirements for XML structures and WebPub capabilities that were needed to publish that part of the journal. The team committed to building that functionality into an increment of potentially shippable product functionality during the next Sprint.

I then met with the next three journal teams. At these meetings, the Product Owner, the XML member, and the WebPub member from the first journal team reviewed their team's Product Backlog and explained the functional and nonfunctional requirements it addressed. The other three editors, or Product Owners, agreed to adopt this Product Backlog for their own journals after updating it to make it specific to the particularities of their publications.

Because each of the three new teams also had part-time members of the XML and WebPub efforts and the XML and WebPub team members had committed to getting a certain amount of XML defined and WebPub capability achieved for the first team within the next Sprint, the three new teams would benefit from the same nonfunctional Product Backlog. Their Sprint tasks built the capabilities that the four journals depended upon. The part-time XML and WebPub team members resolved the dependencies when they returned to their XML and WebPub teams. They were aware of the needs of the individual journal teams and ensured that the functionality to support them was developed in parallel in their XML and WebPub teams.

Lessons Learned

Sometimes projects are so complex that they require something more than the normal implementation of Scrum. In the case of Tree, the dependencies among teams were simply too great for Scrum to handle without some modifications.

I had to go back to thinking about the basics. Scrum is based in empirical process control theory. As the degree of complexity rises, the number of inspections must be increased. Because of the increased frequency of inspections, the opportunity for adaptation also increases. Scrum relies on individual and team commitments rather than on top-down control through planning. Self-organization and human commitment are far more powerful mechanisms than imposed controls, plans, and even loyalty.

At Tree, the complexity was overwhelming, and the situation was nearly chaotic. The XML, WebPub, and journal teams were all developing dependent functionality in parallel. Their Sprint increment functionality was heavily inter-twined and interdependent. Scrum's usual mechanisms for inspections and adaptation would have been overwhelmed if I had constituted the teams as usual: one for XML, one for WebPub, and one team for each journal. The Daily Scrum wouldn't offer enough opportunities for inspection of progress and detection of dependencies at play, and inspection is required for the necessary adaptations to be selected and implemented.

The key modification to Scrum in this case was the alteration of team con-stitution. I populated the teams so that each team included someone who was familiar with each component of this complex situation and had the authority to influence it. The XML part-time team member would commit to the part of XML that was needed to support the increment of journal functionality in the Sprint. The WebPub part-time team member would do the same. Because they were part of the journal teams as well as the XML and WebPub teams, these individ-uals were responsible for coordinating the product development that the journal, XML, and WebPub product teams accomplished during each Sprint. These people then went back to their XML and WebPub teams and ensured that the teams built only functionality that met the needs of the journal teams. At the same time, they synchronized the work of the journal teams with that of XML and WebPub teams. This cross-team coordination is very similar to what later became known as a Scrum of Scrums, in which the work of many teams is coor-dinated by individuals from each of the teams. This worked well at Tree, and trade journals started appearing within three months with a rapid ramp-up of the rest of the journals thereafter.

The Situation at Lapsec

The United States became aware of its vulnerability to terrorism on September 11, 2001. Suddenly, vectors of seemingly unrelated activities coalesced. One ques-tion we persistently ask is how could we have been unaware of this threat? From all of the data collected daily, couldn't a pattern have been detected, a threat perceived, and a warning issued? Indeed, massive amounts of data are collected daily by government agencies in the United States at federal, state, and local levels. However, little of this data is used for more than supporting a single institution or its initial goals. Privacy concerns and an absence of clear need had previously deterred attempts to convert this data into pertinent, widely shared information.

The possibility of deriving such information from masses of disparate data had been the subject of research at Lapsec for several years. Lapsec referred to the technique as *data fusion*. Data fusion applied advanced algorithms to large quantities of data, rapidly reduced it into globs with consequences, and finally stored it as information that could be subjected to pattern analysis. Lapsec received the go-ahead for this project in early 2002. At the same time, Lapsec was granted access to all of the transactional databases supporting various levels of American government.

The project not only had complexities, but resolving each complexity required different levels of skill, intensity, and persistence. Timely data had to be continuously extracted from agencies that didn't know the meaning of the word "cooperation." This data had to be carefully filtered and reduced to minimize extraction, transfer, and load times. Algorithms had to be constructed to browse, search, parse, correlate, and store intermediate results. New data technologies had to be acquired or created to store the intermediate data in dynamically changing data structures. Last, data fusion algorithms had to be employed to identify and highlight the needles in the haystack that could represent threats to national security.

This project was a first for Lapsec in many ways: the technologies involved in this project were untested, and the degree of cooperation required was higher than ever before. Accordingly, the first milestone was a proof of concept. Experts on algorithm, database, and fusion technologies and developers were brought together to form a team to reach this milestone.

The team members struggled for several weeks without making much progress. The unknowns and interdependencies were simply too great. How much data should they initially acquire? Which agencies should they approach for data feeds? How could they quickly acquire the requisite data storage capabilities? Would a commercial data storage facility work, or would they have to build their own? What kind of algorithms should they develop? After several weeks of struggling, the team decided they needed a process that would focus their efforts. Several team members knew of Scrum and suggested that the team try it.

I had doubts about whether Scrum would be able to help resolve the situation. In most complex projects, I'm able to make timely suggestions because I see patterns that I recognize from my previous experiences. This project, however, was classified: I wasn't allowed to know anything about it. Most of what I thought I knew about the requirements of the project I'd inferred rather than been told explicitly. It is entirely possible that my inferences are incorrect and the project was an effort to catch salmon poachers!

Application of Scrum

I offer a service called Project Quickstart. It is a two-day exercise that gets a new project team unfamiliar with Scrum launched on its project. During Project Quickstart, I teach the team about Scrum, and I help the team go through a Sprint planning meeting for their project. At the end of the Quickstart, the team has begun its first Sprint, and the first increment of product functionality is due in 30 calendar days.

After the first day of Quickstart with the Lapsec team, I was frustrated. I didn't feel that they really understood Scrum. The day felt like a formal training exercise, not the start of the team's first Sprint. Team members were still acting like people from different organizations who were investigating something new. They didn't act like a self-organizing team performing as a single unit to solve a problem.

How could I help them? Every time I tried to get them to discuss their goals and Product Backlog, they told me they would have to shoot me if they told me. Lapsec had decided that progress in the project was so urgent that there wasn't enough time to get me enough security clearance to learn the basics of the project. At least, that's what they told me—perhaps I had failed the security clearance! In any case, the team couldn't tell me anything about its work. Some information was unintentionally passed on nonetheless. The team felt secure enough to tell me about the project's data fusion algorithms, the functions of its host organizations, and its merging of a lot of disparate governmental data.

For Scrum to work, the team has to deeply and viscerally understand collective commitment and self-organization. Scrum's theory, practices, and rules are easy to grasp intellectually. But until a group of individuals has made a collective commitment to deliver something tangible in a fixed amount of time, those individuals probably don't get Scrum. When the team members stop acting as many and adopt and commit to a common purpose, the team becomes capable of self-organization and can quickly cut through complexity and produce actionable plans. At that point, the members of a team no longer accept obstacles, but instead scheme, plot, noodle, and brainstorm about how to remove them. They figure out how to make their project happen despite the different backgrounds and skill sets each person brings to the job.

I couldn't sleep for fear that the next day might be a disaster and the training session as a whole might fail. Finally, I decided that I had enough information to construct a hypothetical project. I had been told the vision of the project was to improve national security through the merging and fusing of data. I knew some of the people were national data experts, others were mathematicians responsible for algorithm design, and still others were Internet search experts. Every U.S. citizen was familiar with the criticisms of the government regarding intelligence gathering and usage prior to 9/11. Even though I would probably be wrong about the details, I felt that I could probably construct an adequate hypothetical Product Backlog to help the team meld.

The next morning, I started by reviewing the concepts of Product Backlog and sashimi with the team. I then passed out the hypothetical Product Backlog that I had written the previous night. I asked the team to spend the next two hours going over it and selecting the work for the first Sprint. I told them that after two hours they would have to tell me what Product Backlog they had selected to turn into a full, demonstrable increment of potentially shippable product functionality during the first Sprint. In other words, what could they accomplish? I hoped my hypothetical Product Backlog might be close enough to their real project to make the class seem real to this team.

The Product Backlog consisted of one functional requirement and a number of supporting nonfunctional requirements. The requirements held that the product ought to be able to perform the following functions:

- Identify those people who have attended flight school over the past three months and who fit the profile of someone who might intend to commit an act of terror against the United States.

- Present information in a graphical manner that leads to intuitive exploration through such techniques as merging and drill down.

- Combine information from multiple sources correlated in relationship to the inquiry or criteria being posed.

- Deconstruct an inquiry into relevant data.

- Provide intermediate storage of extracted data in such a manner that it could be readily codified and later used. Do this dynamically as the inquiries are parsed and without undue intervention by the person making the inquiry.

By combining the requirements to demonstrate just one piece of functionality within the time limit of the Sprint, Scrum forced the team to focus its attention on the immediate. I told the team that I was their Product Owner and would answer any questions regarding the Product Backlog and project. Then I told the teams to start work.

As the exercise progressed, the team laid out tentative designs, explored the amount of data that could be retrieved, analyzed the elements and attributes required to support the required functionality, and designed several simple fusion algorithms. They struggled with how they could limit the work. How could they do all of this work and still produce sashimi in one Sprint? Under the pressure of the Sprint time limit, the team realized that it had to use a one-time extract of data from the source databases. It didn't have time to build formal database interfaces. The team came to realize that it needed to put only representative pieces of the whole product together to produce the desired functionality. There was no need for the team to build every piece of the product.

At the end of the two hours, the team described what it could do. The team had collaborated with me, the Product Owner, to devise something of value that could be done in one Sprint. In the process, the team members had self-organized and become a single cohesive team. The team had gone from being a separate group of individuals at a class to a team committed to finding a solution. The team had learned the essence of the Scrum process!

The rest of the day was spent constructing a hypothetical Sprint goal and Sprint Backlog. Most pleasing to me, team members from different organizations devised Sprint Backlog items that required cross-functional responsibilities that would require significant cooperation to complete. By the end of the day, I was satisfied. I felt that the team had grasped Scrum. I felt that the team members knew how to plan and commit well enough to do so in the future without any help from me.

I asked the team to spend the next day on real work. Its first step would be to modify the hypothetical Product Backlog into an actual project Product Backlog. Then the team would repeat the Sprint planning meeting with live Product Backlog, spending two hours designing and constructing a Sprint Backlog for the real project. I asked the team to call me if it had any questions that I could answer—at least, questions that I could answer without getting security clearance.

I got e-mail from the person who engaged me for the Project Quickstart. He related the team's success the next day and its successful initiation of the first Sprint. But I haven't heard from the team since. My e-mails go unanswered. I presume the team is alive and well, producing something that makes me secure but is too secret for me to know about. Sometimes I wonder whether I was the only person in the room who was using his real name!

Lessons Learned

We can see that the ScrumMaster has to be effective regardless of the circumstances. Although ScrumMasters might be tempted to think of themselves as powerful, they are really only enablers. My hands were tied at Lapsec by my lack of knowledge of the application and the technology. My suggestions were based on mere guesswork. It's one thing to read and talk about Scrum, but it's another to implement it. Scrum must be put into place before it can be fully understood.

The dynamics of self-organization, collaboration, and emergence are best understood when a team faces a real problem. My description of Scrum remained merely academic for the team until I provided the team with a hypothetical Product Backlog that was similar enough to its own backlog of work that team members could get emotionally involved with it and feel as though they were making real progress. At that point, everyone's understanding of Scrum quickly moved from intellectual to experiential. From then on, the team was able to employ Scrum's practices and rules to reduce the complexity of its situation to something that could be addressed within a 30-day Sprint.

Conclusions

The Service1st, Tree, and Lapsec projects were all so complex that the usual project planning and control practices had failed. All of the projects required the close synchronization of multiple activities. All of the projects had multiple teams working simultaneously to produce a demonstrable product within a short period of time. And all of them were floundering as the teams tried to figure out how they should start and how they should recast their situations and create actionable plans.

Out-of-the-box Scrum doesn't have practices that address the complexities of every project. However, ScrumMasters have only to refer back to Scrum theory to find Scrum practices that can be readily adapted to handle even the most complex projects.

The thread running through the Service1st, Tree, and Lapsec projects was self-organization. The complexity of the situation was too great for individuals to be able to settle on a plan of action. My job was to that of a coach or a mentor. I taught the teams how to deal with increasing levels of complexity through self-organization within and supported by the practices of Scrum. I reduced the complexity to a degree where the team could cope and function. I helped staff the team with people who had all of the skills needed to understand the complexity and commit to resolving it.

In the Service1st project, I reduced the confusion in the situation by focusing the team on just the next 30 calendar days. I asked the team to take one piece of functionality and figure out how to make it work. I asked the team to forget the rest of the release and to focus on a few concrete steps, assuring them that the rest would fall into place. I gave them permission to ignore their task-based assignments in the meantime. The team was able to focus and implement the foundation upon which the rest of the release and future Sprints depended.

In the Tree project, I reduced the complexity of the situation by staffing the teams so that all the expertise necessary to develop a piece of functionality was included within each team. Each team would be able to resolve any dependencies it had on other teams. Most members of each team were able to focus on the work at hand, while the cross-team members spent time synchronizing team progress with that of other dependent teams.

In the Lapsec project, I had to help the team practice Scrum. Lecturing on Scrum theory and practices proved inadequate in this instance. Until the team actually used Scrum to solve some of the problems it was facing, the team wouldn't really grasp Scrum. By providing the team with an example similar to its real work, I broke through to the team and helped it understand how to use Scrum. When they entered the Sprint time-box with a real problem to solve, the team members attacked it like a pack of wild dogs. The time-box works well— as Mark Twain once said, "Nothing focuses the mind like a noose."

The ScrumMaster applies Scrum theory to projects with different types and degrees of complexity. In every instance in which they apply Scrum, Scrum-Masters will be called upon to apply their understanding to a project's aims and difficulties so that the ScrumMaster aptly supports the team's efforts to achieve those aims.

5

The Product Owner

The ScrumMaster is responsible for removing any barriers between the development Teams and the Product Owner and customers so that the customers can directly drive development. The ScrumMaster is also responsible for showing the Product Owner how to use Scrum to maximize project return on investment (ROI) and meet the project's objectives.

Neither of these responsibilities is easy to fulfill. The ScrumMaster often has to work against 20 years of history during which customers and Teams have drifted apart. Each sees the other as a source of something that is of great value but that is also extremely hard to get. The customer knows from experience how unlikely it is that the Team will deliver a system, much less a system that meets the customer's needs. The Team knows from experience that the customer is fickle, always changing his or her mind just when the Team thinks it knows what to build. Together, they believe there is little opportunity to work closely together to each other's mutual benefit.

"Scrum solved my customer involvement problem," is a refrain that I've heard from IT executives over the years. Scrum provides many opportunities for resolving this industry-wide problem. The Team and the Product Owner should be constantly collaborating, scheming together about how to get the most value for the business from the selected technologies. Once implemented, Scrum practices facilitate collaboration between customers and development Teams in the normal course of a Scrum project. We'll examine strategies and tactics for the ScrumMaster to bring this collaboration about using stealth, if necessary. Let's look at how Scrum helped solve the customer involvement problem without either the customers or the Team knowing that Scrum was being employed.

Customer and Team Collaboration

When I started developing software, customer involvement and collaboration weren't problems. In the 1960s, the computers were less powerful, the users were fewer, the applications were simpler, and the idea of milestones was still unknown. I used short iterations of one or two days. I'd meet with the customer, and we'd sketch out on paper what he or she wanted. We'd discuss the problem until I understood it. Then I'd go to my desk, design and code the solution, punch up the cards, and compile the program. Once the compile and link were clean, I'd run some test data against the program. Then I'd return to the customer and ask, "Is this what you wanted?" We didn't realize it at the time, but this was heaven.

As the applications and technology became more complex and the number of stakeholders in a project increased, practices were inserted to coordinate the communication among the increased numbers of participants. For instance, because many stakeholders were involved, we began to collect all of their requirements prior to starting development. We felt that the system should implement the sum of their respective requirements. Because documentation was such an inadequate medium of communicating, we started to use pictures to communicate, supporting these pictures with text. And because pictures were imprecise, we developed modeling techniques to formally represent the pictures. Each step drove a wedge between the stakeholders and the developers. We went from face-to-face communication to documentation. We went from quick turnaround to lengthy requirements-gathering phases. We went from simple language to artifacts that were arcane and highly specialized.

In retrospect, the more we improved the practice of software engineering, the further we widened the gap between stakeholders and developers. The last step in the estrangement was the introduction of *waterfall methodology*, which embodies all the flaws of sequential development. Waterfall methodology gathers all the requirements, then creates the design, then writes the code, then develops and runs tests, and finally implements the system. Between each of these steps, or phases, were review meetings. Stakeholders were invited to these meetings to review the progress to date. At these meetings, developers and managers would ask customers, "Do these requirements that we've gathered and the models that demonstrate them constitute a full and accurate representation of what you want? Because once you say yes, it will be increasingly expensive for you to change your mind!" As you can see, this wording implies a contract between the customers and the developers. By this point, there was little in-person collaboration; in its place were contracts that said, "If you agree that what I showed you is the complete description of your requirements, we will proceed. If you don't agree, we'll continue to develop requirements until you give up!"

A favorite ScrumMaster of mine used to say, "What does that have to do with code?" Anything that didn't quickly and demonstrably lead to code was a waste of time in her eyes. Her attitude drove the requirements modelers nuts. They felt that it was a wholly unprofessional viewpoint. However, it did cause them to evaluate everything they did in terms of immediate stakeholder value.

One of the ingredients of Scrum is a practice known as *sashimi*. Sashimi is a Japanese delicacy consisting of thin slices of raw fish. Each slice is complete in itself, a complete taste similar to the way every other slice tastes. Scrum uses the sashimi technique to require that every slice of functionality created by the developers be complete. All of the requirements gathering and analysis, design work, coding, testing, and documentation that constitute a complete product are required to be completed in every Sprint and demonstrated in the Sprint increment of functionality. Sprints are kept short enough that the stakeholders don't lose interest in the project before the Sprints are completed. And stakeholders can see that they have an opportunity to redirect the project at the start of every Sprint to optimize the value they derive from the project. At the end of every Sprint, stakeholders see new functionality. Models, requirements, and internal artifacts might be of use to the developers, but they are never shown to the stakeholders.

Stakeholders tend to be skeptical when first told about Scrum. Customers have had so many "silver bullets" imposed on them that they can be forgiven for this, especially since each of the silver bullets involved more work for them but fewer results. A primary tool the ScrumMaster can use to improve customer involvement is the delivery of quick results that customers can potentially use in their organization. The Sprint planning and Sprint review meetings are the bookends to initiate and fulfill this expectation. If the Team is at all capable and the project is technologically feasible, the stakeholders and Product Owner can't wait to collaborate more with the Team.

Let's look at some instances in which Scrum provided an opportunity for the Product Owner and development Teams to work closely together to maximize the value of the project. At Service1st, we'll see how top management recognized the opportunity to get directly involved as Product Owners. At TechCore, we'll see how a young entrepreneur was able to sell his company for a premium by focusing his efforts on his work as the Product Owner. Finally, at MegaBank, we'll see how the ScrumMaster got the customers to be the Product Owners while minimizing the work necessary to teach and implement Scrum.

Getting Service1st's Management Back in Action

As I have mentioned, systems development used to be simpler. But as the complexity of the systems in question and the environment in which they are being developed has increased, people and organizations have lost their way.

We visited Service1st in Chapter 2 and Chapter 4. Service1st used a defined project management process that included Gantt charts, resource allocation, and time reporting to plan, initiate, and track project progress. Reports were sent to top management that indicated the critical paths, percentage of work completed, and other key project metrics. Management didn't feel that was enough, however, and also required the vice president of development to report in person at a weekly executive meeting.

Service1st's two top executives, Tom and Hank, had started the company and were among its first programmers. As Service1st grew, they realized that they had to give up day-to-day control of development and delegate authority to others. As a result, they were increasingly frustrated when releases began to slip more often and the product quality decreased. Everything seemed fine until the last two months of the release cycle rolled around. Then, without warning, everyone was working overtime to get the release out. The bug count kept climbing—often, it was all the developers could do to keep the bug count at a releasable, yet lamentable, level. Service1st decided to adopt Scrum and see whether the situation could be improved during the next release cycle.

Sprint Review Meeting

Seven teams were sprinting; they concluded their Sprints on the same date so that their Sprint reviews could be simultaneous. The standard format for the Sprint review meeting was modified so that management could find out how all of the teams were doing at a given point in time. The teams took over a quality assurance (QA) laboratory for a day. Each team claimed a territory in the laboratory and set it up in preparation for the demonstration of their increments of functionality. The teams organized their presentation areas as though they were presenting at a conference, hanging signs with their team names from the ceiling and posting the Sprint goal and Product Backlog on the wall. Chairs were placed in front of the workstation, and evaluation forms were available for feedback. Essentially, seven vendors, or teams, were presenting their wares. Although this involved more preparation that I usually like to see with Scrum, it established an upbeat mood that raised energy levels and motivation.

The vice president of development brought all of top management to the Sprint review meeting in the QA laboratory. A member of each team stood and briefed management on the team name, its Sprint goal, and the Product Backlog it had selected and would be demonstrating and then summarized what had gone right during the Sprint, as well as what had gone wrong. This prepared top management for what they were about to see.

Management walked from team to team for functionality demonstrations. The teams then answered questions and recorded suggestions that they factored into the Product Backlog for their next Sprints. This collaboration between management and development teams went on for several hours. The teams then again took turns summarizing the work they'd done. Each team took about 10 minutes to report on what enhancements had been suggested to them. They asked whether they had missed anything, entertained further discussion, and then wrapped up.

Lessons Learned

The teams turned the Sprint review into a formal Sprint reporting mechanism. Because they really understood the value of face-to-face communication over documentation, they replaced reports with collaboration. By selecting a conference format, the team created an opportunity to collaborate with management for more than three hours. Management was delighted. Unlike a report, this collaboration wasn't static and sterile. Instead, it was a vibrant demonstration of a reality.

After the Sprint review, some of top management gathered to comment on the Sprint review meeting. The vice president of marketing said, "I thought it was great. I was able to see exactly where you were. Can I get a demo of this to show customers? Can I bring customers to the next Sprint review meeting?" Most telling was a comment from Tom, one of the cofounders, who said, "When we were small, we used to have this all of the time. But as we got bigger, we lost the ability to keep everyone directly involved in our choice of direction. This is a way we can work together again."

Fixing the Problem of XFlow at MegaFund

I used to refer to Geoff, the product manager of the XFlow workflow system that powers all of MegaFund's business operations, as the "shadow Product Owner." We first met MegaFund in Chapter 3. Geoff used Scrum at MegaFund, but no one knew it. Here's what Geoff had to say about his experience as an undercover Product Owner:

A big reason for my success this year was my involvement with Scrum through you and Jack. It must have been November of last year when both of you told me to meet with customers every 30 days. That monthly meeting has become the model for successful organizations at MegaFund. All of the XFlow customers rave about how involved they are with engineering and how they know exactly what we are working on at all times, as well as about our on-time delivery. Other organizations are now trying to put together these types of meetings to bolster their communication with their customers.

How did Geoff manage to implement Scrum without telling anyone? For that matter, why did he do so? I'll answer both questions in this section.

XFlow was developed internally by MegaFund from the licensed source code of a commercial workflow product. As the XFlow engineering team customized the product to MegaFund's needs, it became the arterial system for MegaFund's information and workflow. The engineering team, located in Salt Lake City, enhanced and maintained XFlow for MegaFund companies worldwide. Emboldened by the internal success of XFlow, the engineering team planned to market it externally and begin selling it to other companies. Unfortunately, this decision created a tension between the engineering group and the internal customers. The engineering group prioritized enhancements that made XFlow more commercially viable, while the internal customers prioritized enhancements and bug fixes that solved their operational problem. Over several years, the two groups grew deeply distrustful of each other. Several of the larger business units of MegaFund started investigating the possibility of replacing XFlow with new commercial products. These internal customers felt that external vendors might be more responsive to their needs than the internal XFlow engineering group had proven. This was a potential catastrophe. If the internal customers implemented other workflow systems, interfaces would have to be built to accommodate them. The MegaFund workflow would become less than seamless. Furthermore, losing some internal customers would hurt the remaining internal customers by decreasing the funds available to enhance and sustain XFlow.

The politics heated up as individual companies escalated their causes. It seemed that a solution would be very difficult to find. The MegaFund Scrum-Master, Jack, and I sat down to brainstorm with Geoff. Did Scrum offer anything that could help him and save XFlow? We focused on the Sprint review and Sprint planning meetings. Would it help if Geoff facilitated a meeting like these for the engineers and customers? Neither the engineers nor the customers had given Geoff the authority to create or prioritize a Product Backlog—and they weren't likely to, either—but perhaps he could facilitate a session where this would naturally occur.

Addressing the Problem

Geoff set up an all-day meeting for XFlow engineering management and internal customer management. He told everyone that the purpose of the meeting was to get everyone's concerns aired and to see whether a common ground could be found. He did not mention Scrum. Everyone was so riled up that they were looking for a scapegoat, not a process. Geoff set the agenda: first, engineering would present the product as it had been recently enhanced; second, the internal customers would present their most pressing needs; third, engineering would present its enhancement plans; and fourth, the two groups would see whether there was a common ground.

The customers watched with rancor while the engineers presented their updates to the product. Surely, the customers assumed, the engineers hadn't done anything that would be of use to the customers! But they were surprised; some of the updates were not only useful, but they were also ones that the customers had themselves requested. Then each customer presented his or her most urgent needs. Geoff recorded these on a whiteboard, eliminating duplicates and keeping the wording clear. When the engineers presented their planned enhancements, Geoff factored these into the list on the whiteboard, again eliminating duplicates. As the presentations went forward, it became clear that there was indeed some commonality between the customers' and the engineers' respective agendas.

Geoff told everyone present that he didn't know whether a long-term solution was possible, since the two groups had such conflicting interests. However, he noted, if the engineering team met some of the needs of the internal customers, XFlow would be more commercially viable. These internal customers could potentially be references for external prospects. He then noted that some of the enhancements that the engineering team had presented represented desirable functionality that external workflow vendors were pitching to MegaFund.

Geoff then used a key Scrum tactic. He asked whether the list represented everyone's most urgent needs. He reminded everyone to focus on the immediate future and see whether a near-term game plan could be devised. He asked everyone to help figure out what could be done over the next 30 days that would help everyone the most and do the most to solve everyone's problems. After an hour of mostly collegial discussion, the two groups together selected seven items to develop and some critical bugs to fix. Geoff asked if everyone could wait 30 days to see whether developing these features and fixing these bugs would improve the situation before doing anything rash. Everyone agreed to give it a try.

A month later, the engineering team presented its work. It described the technical problems it had encountered and the way it had worked around them to implement the desired functionality and fix the troublesome bugs. The customers questioned the engineers and asked them to demonstrate various other parts of the functionality. The customers were impressed that the team had done so much work in just 30 days; the team had built completed functionality, not just internal models and other stuff of no interest to these customers. The customers were also pleased that the work done was what they had prioritized; the customers felt that the engineering team had really listened to them. The engineers were pleased that the customers were pleased and no longer out for blood. They had built something that advanced the product commercially and yet satisfied their internal MegaFund customers.

Geoff then handed out the list of most urgent functionality from the prior meeting. He asked for updates from the engineering team and customers. Had anyone's needs changed? Had the external product requirements changed? Had any critical bugs arisen? Geoff led the discussion and then helped the two groups prioritize the list of functionality to develop and bugs to fix and then to select the work the engineers would do during the next 30 days.

Lessons Learned

Geoff wasn't a traditional Scrum Product Owner: he didn't write up a Product Backlog, prioritize it, and meet with the development team at a Sprint planning meeting. Geoff had taken the Scrum expression "the art of the possible" and facilitated direct collaboration between the internal customers and the engineering teams. It turned out that when they met face to face, their needs and problems had significant overlap. All Geoff did was help them get together to explore these needs and problems and then develop a plan for action. Because the plan was to last only 30 days, there was no point bickering over whose problem was to be top priority. Everyone could see that the work to do was being whittled away and that everyone's problems would eventually be addressed. The regular delivery of functionality every 30 days reassured them that their needs weren't being deferred indefinitely.

By applying some of Scrum's practices and philosophies, Geoff was able to resolve a most difficult situation within MegaFund. His evaluation of Scrum, made after two years of experience applying these Scrum techniques at XFlow, reflects how well this commonsense approach worked at MegaFund.

When people don't get together, face to face, and talk to each other, they often project their problems onto each other. The engineering team and internal customers hadn't met for over a year, and their normal mode of communication had devolved until it consisted merely of e-mail messages from one group to the other. When they got together, with Geoff as their facilitator, they were able to set aside their differences and find a common ground. Simple courtesy and good manners is often the grease that makes these meetings work.

Company Goals at TechCore

In this section, we'll see how an executive at TechCore in a mad dash to make a success of his company is unable to keep his priorities straight—until he starts using Scrum. Michel felt as though he had to chase down every lead, but pulling together a Product Backlog enabled him to see that the real money could be made by focusing attention on product development. Within four months of implementing Scrum, he had more than achieved his goals: his company's prospects had improved so much that a previous offer to buy out TechCore was reinstated at a significantly higher amount.

TechCore was one of the many startup telecommunications companies in Boston during the late 1990s. The cry at these companies was "more bandwidth, more capacity," and at TechCore, young PhDs from MIT had the patents and the answers. Using dense wavelength frequency multiplexing and avoiding transitions from light wave to electric at junctures, Michel's company, TechCore, was able to increase capacity by over 4000 percent. Michel hired other bright MIT PhDs to develop his products. Mortals from micromanufacturing, finance, human resources, purchasing, and administration staffed the rest of the company, which was growing as rapidly as people could be hired. The company had recently had a $540 million offer to buy it and its new technology, but Michel and TechCore's investors felt that their company was worth more.

Michel was determined to pull together a subsystem of TechCore's technology that would more clearly demonstrate a greater value at a telecommunications conference and show four months away. Meanwhile, component yields were 1 in 1000, human resources was bringing in the wrong people, finance was busy planning the next expansion, and Michel was trying to be all things to all people, even going so far as to design the cabinet that the subsystem would be demonstrated in at the upcoming show.

How Scrum Helped TechCore

Michel and I pulled together a Product Backlog that focused on things important to the upcoming show; all other work—even improving manufacturing yield—was given a lower priority. Yes, it was important to have sustainable yields, but not if the strategy was to sell the company in the near term. Whoever acquired TechCore would probably have the necessary manufacturing expertise to do so. The exercise of pulling the Product Backlog together was extremely beneficial. Michel had thought that he could do it all. He thought that he could ensure new product delivery while managing every other task being performed at the company. As a result, he was stretched too thin, and he wasn't able to give anything adequate attention. In deciding that product development requirements were higher priority than manufacturing, space planning, and recruiting, Michel was also admitting that he had only limited energy and that he had to decide where to allocate it.

Previously, Michel held daylong review meetings to impart his knowledge and direction to the development engineers. These often degenerated into design sessions on one part of the subsystem, helping only a small segment of the team while chewing up everyone else's time. We decided to get Michel involved through the Daily Scrums. At the Daily Scrums, it became clear that the PhDs weren't talking to each other; they were often stuck on problems that someone else could have helped them solve. Team members began helping each other on a daily basis. And Michel saw ample opportunities to step in and provide necessary and critical assistance. As each engineer reported his or her status, Michel saw that if he focused his attention on product development, he could expedite design decisions, ensure that the correct path was taken, and actually get involved in the critical business of his company. He focused his efforts on helping the team with its short-term problems, which were all related to preparing the subsystem for the show.

One surprising problem that the Daily Scrums made visible took a while for me to understand. It seemed to me that most of the engineers spent inordinate amounts of time acquiring components. They would request components from purchasing and then sit around and wait for them. When the component finally arrived, it often wasn't the one they needed. When I discussed this problem with purchasing, it became clear that this department was also frustrated by the situation. The components that the engineers were requisitioning were new to the market, often little more than preannounced prototypes. The manufacturing yields for these components were low because they used new technologies, and they were also very expensive and hard to locate. The purchasing staff often had to attempt to describe the components to the vendor when they didn't have the technical knowledge that would enable them to do so. The result was a lot of wasted time and frustration. Engineers would ask for a component, purchasing would try to find the part, the vendor would try to provide an alternative component, purchasing would interrupt the engineer to get his advice, and even if the engineer accepted the alternative, by the time purchasing got back to the vendor, the component had often been sold to someone else. This happened every week.

To solve the purchasing problem, we hired two junior engineers to work in the engineering development group. They were "junior" only in the sense that they didn't have PhDs from MIT. A senior engineer would address a request for a part or component to a junior engineer. The junior engineer would then work with purchasing to acquire the most appropriate part as quickly as possible. The junior engineer was empowered to make tradeoffs. To help increase the likelihood that tradeoffs were optimized, all of the engineers were equipped with cell phones. Tradeoffs were made in the real time between the vendor, purchasing, the junior engineer, and—when necessary—the senior engineer who needed the part.

You might think that expediting the purchasing process is a trivial accomplishment. However, the Daily Scrum showed that dealing with purchasing was one of the greatest drains on the team's time. It was keeping the senior engineers from working with each other and with Michel. It also demoralized them because they were getting so little done.

Lessons Learned

Michel's intense participation in product development improved the department's focus exponentially, and it sped critical problems to resolution. Hiring junior engineers as procurement specialists freed the senior engineers to work on difficult problems and simultaneously sped up procurement. The result was a successful demonstration of a subsystem at the show followed by BigTel's $1.43 billion buyout of TechCore a month after the show. Michel's focused participation in the company's highest priority work generated an ROI of almost $1 billion dollars within six months. Not a bad day's work.

Company Goals at MegaBank Funds Transfer System

It isn't always necessary to make a big deal out of the role of Product Owner. Sometimes it makes sense to low-ball the whole thing and propose something casual instead, like getting together and talking about what to do next. People are often suspicious of new jargon and new methodologies—and not without reason. This section's example will highlight the importance of talking to business people in plain language—or at least in business language!

MegaBank is one of the largest financial institutions in the United States, with nationwide branches and enough capitalization to affect monetary markets. MegaBank transferred $39.6 trillion last year within and between its own operations and with other parties. The system that performed these transfers, maintained audit logs, ensured the security of the transactions, and successfully completed all transactions is called Fund Transfer System (FTS). When I arrived on the scene, the FTS project team was gearing up to start work on the second release of FTS. The team's project manager, Pat, wanted to use Scrum. She had heard that Scrum had helped other customers become more involved in development projects; the FTS project needed similar help.

Since the first rollout of FTS, the customers at MegaBank had changed. The manager who had directed the first release of FTS, Henry, had been promoted to another job. Henry's next in command, Mary, had taken over his position, but she found managing bug fixing and enhancements to be time-consuming and of less importance than her other responsibilities. Mary had delegated this work, along with communications and coordination of the project, to her next in command, Laurie, a sharp manager with very limited understanding of MegaFund's FTS functions. Laurie was having a hard time directing project activities.

MegaFund FTS management had established a release date of October 15, and it was already May. How could the FTS team get some solid direction from its customers and collaborate with them about alternative release contents during the interim?

How Scrum Helped FTS

Henry, Mary, and Laurie came to a meeting that Pat set up. Pat told them that the FTS team was going to use Scum, which had already been used to successfully manage other joint projects at MegaBank. Henry, Mary, and Laurie didn't know what this meant to them and how much time was involved. They just hoped that Scrum would help them work more closely with the FTS development team. I was asked to start the meeting by presenting Scrum to Henry, Mary, and Laurie. I made the presentation quick and low-key. I told them that we used a prioritized list of things that they wanted done to drive development cycles of one month. Every month, we'd show them completed functionality, we'd review the list of what to do next, and we'd figure out what the team could do next. Henry, Mary, and Laurie were very pleased; Scrum seemed simple, easy to understand, and it required only a formal meeting every month. They could certainly handle that. They had been concerned that a new development process would involve training, new forms, new reports, and a lot of overhead. In contrast with their expectations, Scrum seemed very straightforward.

We spent the rest of the morning with the development team, reviewing the list of functionality requested for the second release. We created rough time estimates for the development of each item and grouped the items into possible Sprints. "Sprint" was a new term for Henry, Mary, and Laurie, but they relaxed when they learned that it just meant one month. This exercise relieved everyone; Henry, Mary, Laurie, and the development team felt that the workload was known, under control, and potentially achievable within 30 days. They had collaborated and reached a tentative plan in language common to both sides. We had set aside the entire afternoon to figure out what to do in the next Sprint. However, the team, working with Mary and Laurie, was able to select the Product Backlog in an hour. The team then got to work building the Sprint Backlog, while Henry, Mary, and Laurie went back to their offices, comfortable that progress was being made on the next release.

Lessons Learned

I downplayed Scrum to the FTS team and management. They needed to learn to talk to each other in a common language. Product Backlog requirements were the language in question, and everything fell in place once they began speaking in that language. Neither side needed to learn the Scrum language and process; they started using it only as a way of describing how they were going to collaborate. A Product Backlog was just their prioritized list of requirements. A month was the time between meetings, and it didn't really matter whether they called it something funny like a "Sprint." The FTS team has been using Scrum for over six months, delivering releases and collaborating with its counterpart teams. Downplaying Scrum simplified this collaboration by reducing the overhead of learning something new and the apprehension of a strange new methodology.

Conclusions

We've looked at four examples of a key customer stepping forward to direct the development of software or a product. Through the use of Scrum, each has taken over the role of Product Owner—some knowingly and others unknowingly. In each case, they have learned to collaborate with the Team, Sprint by Sprint, to control the direction and impact of the development effort.

In each case, the ScrumMaster has brought the Product Owner and the Team together. The collaboration has been either explicit or clandestine, but in each case, it was successful. A key element in each example is that the Team and the Product Owner learned to understand each other. Although this might seem easy, the Team and the Product Owner were in fact speaking different languages before Scrum was implemented. The Product Owner had learned to talk in terms of business requirements and objectives, whereas the Team had learned to speak in terms of technology. Because the Product Owner is unlikely to learn the technology, one of the main jobs of the ScrumMaster is to teach the Team to talk in terms of business needs and objectives. The common denominator between the Team and the Product Owner is the Product Backlog.

I have conducted a number of classes over the last year to teach people to become effective ScrumMasters. These classes are referred to as Certified ScrumMaster training. In addition to figuring out how to apply Scrum to various individual situations, we've addressed how the ScrumMaster can get the Product Owner and the Team to speak the same language, to use a meaningful common vocabulary to discuss a mutual problem. The attendees are grouped into teams, and they get together to discuss a business problem and present their understanding and recommendations to the Product Owner. These teams almost always present their understanding in "technospeak," a language of technology incomprehensible to the Product Owner. When this happens, I show them what they've done and help them learn to do otherwise. Through these exercises, I've ruthlessly helped future ScrumMasters understand the depths of the language divide that has separated customers and developers. Bridging this gap is critical; if both sides can't speak the same language, collaboration can't and won't occur. The Product Owner has no interest in bridging the gap, and doesn't have the background to do so anyway, so it is up to the ScrumMaster to help the Team bridge the gap.

In each of the examples in this chapter, the Product Owner and the Team have collaborated to do the best for the business. Each collaboration has resulted in an improved ROI. But how much of an improvement? Without a benchmark against which to measure, such an achievement remains anecdotal. In the next chapter, we will look at how people at the Certified Scrum-Master classes respond when a benchmark for evaluating the ROI of decisions is in place.

6

Planning a Scrum Project

The Scrum planning process sets stakeholders' expectations. These stakeholders include those who fund the project, those who intend to use the functionality created by the project, and those who will be otherwise affected by the project. The plan is a way of synchronizing stakeholders' expectations with the Team's expectations. In the case of stakeholders who will be users of project functionality, the plan helps them organize their work so that they can be ready to take advantage of the functionality as it is implemented. In the case of stakeholders who are funding the project, the plan details their expectation of what funding is required and when the benefits of the project should be realized. The plan is also the basis of project reporting. At the end of the Sprint, the stakeholders attend the Sprint review meetings and compare the project's actual progress against its planned progress. Changes in course and revisions to the plan made in Sprint planning meetings are explained to the stakeholders. For those who are unable to attend the Sprint review meeting, the project reports compare actual results to the plan—both the original plan and the plan as it has been modified since the project's inception.

The Scrum planning process involves resolving three questions:

- What can those funding the project expect to have changed when the project is finished?

- What progress will have been made by the end of each Sprint?

- Why should those being asked to fund the project believe that the project is a valuable investment, and why should they believe that those proposing the project can deliver those predicted benefits?

Scrum projects require less planning than typical Gantt chart–based projects because those working to deliver the expected benefits provide visibility into their progress at the end of every Sprint. Since Scrum projects are too complex to be described in great detail at their inception, we instead monitor them and guide them so that they will deliver the best possible results.

The minimum plan necessary to start a Scrum project consists of a vision and a Product Backlog. The vision describes why the project is being undertaken and what the desired end state is. For a system used internally within an organization, the vision might describe how the business operation will be different when the system is installed. For software that is being developed for external sale, the vision might describe the software's major new features and functions, how they will benefit customers, and what the anticipated impact on the marketplace will be. The Product Backlog defines the functional and non-functional requirements that the system should meet to deliver the vision, prioritized and estimated. The Product Backlog is parsed into potential Sprints and releases, as illustrated in Figure 6-1.

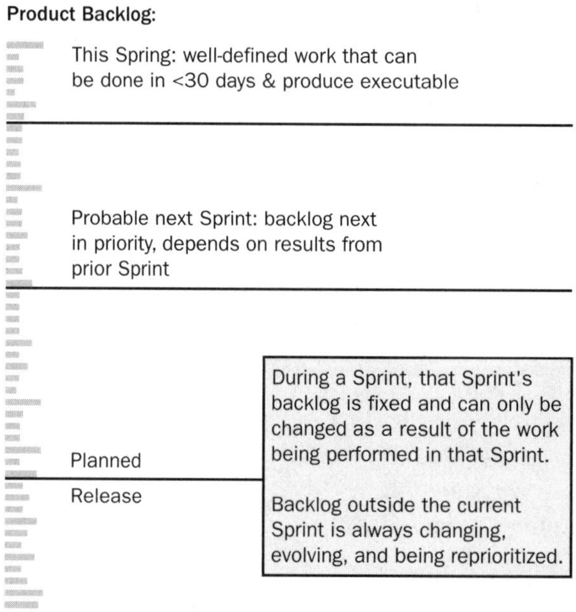

Product Backlog:

This Spring: well-defined work that can be done in <30 days & produce executable

Probable next Sprint: backlog next in priority, depends on results from prior Sprint

Planned

Release

During a Sprint, that Sprint's backlog is fixed and can only be changed as a result of the work being performed in that Sprint.

Backlog outside the current Sprint is always changing, evolving, and being reprioritized.

Figure 6-1   Product Backlog

One of the purposes of the plan is to convince someone to fund the project. The plan should provide sufficient details to satisfy a source of funding that the project has merit, that it will deliver certain things at certain times, that the benefits outweigh the costs and risks, and that the people who will staff the project are sufficiently compentent to execute the plan.

Scrum is often implemented well after the project in question has been planned. In the case of these projects, the funding is already in place and expectations have already been established. What's necessary now is to replan the project in light of Scrum so that the Team, Product Owner, and stakeholders can envision the project as a series of Sprints that lead to a release, all driven by the Product Backlog. The first task is to create the Scrum artifact needed for managing a Scrum project: the Product Backlog. The following section describes an example of such a project.

Managing Cash at MegaBank

MegaBank is one of the largest financial institutions in the world. We'll consider MegaBank's use of Scrum here and in subsequent chapters. Two years after Scrum was first introduced at MegaBank, 20 percent of all MegaBank software projects now use Scrum. One team had heard what a success Scrum had been in other parts of MegaBank and wanted to try it on a pilot project that involved moving one of MegaBank's applications from mainframe systems to the Web. The application in question, known as the "cash application," was used for recording and reporting cash transfers. Funding had been approved, the team had been formed, and the plan had been written. The team was given a memorandum that stated that the Web-based version of the cash application would be complete and ready for implementation in five months. No more details were necessary because the new application would be a one-to-one replica of its mainframe predecessor; consequently, no new functionality had been authorized for this project.

Sprints usually begin with a one-day Sprint planning meeting. For projects like this one, however, I add an additional day to construct a Product Backlog for the project as well to teach the new ScrumMaster, Product Owner, and Team how Scrum works. I find these two-day sessions to be particularly effective for teaching Scrum—in large part because the subject of the lesson is inherently practical, concerning real work that has to be done in the very near term.

The Two-Day Sprint Planning Meeting

The team consisted of five developers. The Product Owner, Julie, was at this meeting, as were Tom, the ScrumMaster, and Ed, the systems development manager. I taught the basics of Scrum—the kinds of things covered in Chapter 1 of this book—for the first three hours of the meeting. Then I told everyone that we were almost ready to start the regular Sprint planning meeting; the only thing we were missing was the Product Backlog. Julie needed a Product Backlog list so that she could identify the highest priority backlog. The team needed to see the Product Backlog list so that it could commit to transforming it into an increment of product functionality. I assured everyone that we'd have the Product Backlog done by the end of the day, but everyone groaned nonetheless.

Team members in particular saw this exercise as unnecessary overhead. They asked why we couldn't just figure out what to do for the next Sprint. After all, that was what being agile was about, they reasoned. I told the team that we needed to get a handle on the project within the context of Scrum; we would be using the Product Backlog to lay down a baseline of expectations against which management at MegaBank could plot the project's progress.

We taped flip-chart paper to the wall and started listing all of the functions in the existing mainframe system, all of which were to be replicated on the Web. We also thought through some nonfunctional requirements, such as establishing a quality assurance (QA) and production environment for the system. Within two hours, we had listed pretty much all of the Product Backlog, and certainly the most important elements. The rest could emerge as we proceeded; we had enough to start with.

Estimating the Product Backlog

The next step was to estimate how much work would be involved in fulfilling the requirements in the Product Backlog. The team members groaned again, assuming that this task would take forever. They doubted that they could come up with accurate estimates—particularly estimates that were accurate enough to correctly set expectations and guide their selection of Product Backlog at every future Sprint. Before we proceeded with estimating, we discussed the nature of complexity and its impact on software development. To estimate each requirement precisely, we would have to know the exact composition and interaction of the requirement, the technology used to build the requirement, and the skills and mood of the people doing the work. We could potentially spend more time trying to define these attributes and their interactions than we would spend actually transforming the requirement into functionality. Worse yet, even if we did so, the nature of complex problems would ultimately render our efforts worthless. The nature of complex problems is such that very small variations in any aspect of the problem can cause extremely large and unpredictable variations in how the problem manifests itself. So no matter how much time we spent improving the accuracy of our estimates, the estimates would still be wildly inaccurate.

After we'd had this discussion, I asked Julie and the team to take a crack at the estimates, bearing in mind the following guideline: the purpose of estimating is to get a handle on the size of each requirement, both in its own right and relative to the size of the other requirements. This information would help us prioritize the Product Backlog and divide it into Sprints. I reminded them that Scrum is empirical and ultimately based on the "art of the possible." The team had only to do its best during each Sprint, and we would then update our expectations about what could be done by the end of each Sprint. We would track actual progress on each Sprint's Product Backlog to determine and project progress on the project as a whole. From this projection, we could predict when the system would be ready for release. In this case, management expected the system to be ready in five months. We would now take a first stab at determining whether this was a realistic expectation. At the end of every Sprint, we would update the expectations by tracking actual delivery of functionality against expected delivery of functionality.

With these guidelines in mind, the team was able to estimate all of the Product Backlog in just one hour. The team based its estimates on its knowledge of the current mainframe cash application—which all the team members had worked on—and team members' understanding of J2EE, Java, and the new technologies that they would be employing. The team, Julie, Tom, and Ed were eager to see how these estimates compared with management expectations: did these estimates indicate that the project would be done in five months? Ed was particularly interested because he was the one who had predicted as much.

What Does "Done" Mean?

Before we proceeded, I asked the team what information its estimates included. Did the estimates take into account how long it would take to analyze, design, and code the requirements in the Product Backlog? Did they include time for unit testing? Were the unit tests automated on something like JUnit? Did the estimates allow time for code reviews, for refactoring, for writing code cleanly and legibly, and for removing unnecessary code? It was important that everyone understood exactly what the estimates allowed for because understanding would prevent people from thinking work was "done" before all of the work taken into account in the estimate was complete. Julie wanted to know why I wanted to discuss this. I told her that the functionality being developed would be more or less valuable according to what work the team performed before considering a requirement fulfilled. For instance, if the team didn't unit test the functionality, we should probably count on finding more bugs later on. If this were the case, we ought to allocate more time for testing of the application prior to implementation because we'd have more bugs to fix. Similarly, if the team was refactoring code as it worked, it would be easier to fix bugs in the future—and the application would be easier to maintain and enhance.

Julie wasn't familiar with JUnit; one of the team members told her that it was an automated testing facility on which the team could build a suite of automated tests to run against the application. Whenever a new piece of code was added, the team would immediately know whether it broke any other pieces of functionality. Julie was fascinated. She wanted a tested and maintainable application, not something that was coded too quickly. She had always assumed that this was what was being delivered and was glad that she now had an opportunity to let the team know that was what she expected. I asked the team to now reestimate all of the Product Backlog with this new knowledge of Julie's expectations. After spending an hour figuring out the impact of this new definition of "done," the team had updated the estimates. Julie then discussed the Product Backlog with the team. Which requirements should be tackled first? Because QA wasn't part of the team, what work could be completed as a unit and given to QA to start testing at the end of every Sprint? What nonfunctional requirements had to be prioritized? The result of this collaboration was the prioritized Product Backlog.

How Hard It Is to Change

It was time to plan what the Team would do over the course of the first Sprint and subsequent Sprints. We estimated how much time on average the team members had available every month. We added this up to get a rough feel for how much time the Team could devote to each Sprint. Then, starting at the top of the Product Backlog, we identified how many items could be potentially included in the first Sprint. We continued down the Product Backlog, estimating potential Sprint contents until the entire Product Backlog was parsed into seven Sprints.

We all sat back. Ed had promised that the Team would deliver the system in five months. Our rough calculations indicated the system would be ready in seven months. Nobody said it, but we all knew that the new definition of "done" contributed to the additional two months. If we had stuck with the Team's first estimates, we might have ended up with an estimate of five months. And if the Team hadn't worked according to this new definition of "done," it might well have delivered the system in five months. But because Julie now understood what "done" meant, the extra time was required. I looked at Julie and asked her whether she wanted us to go back to the old estimates. Julie was upset. She wanted to know how we had committed to five months if we knew that we would be delivering a substandard system. I told Julie that we hadn't known, that until this planning session we couldn't actually predict one way or another.

However, Ed had agreed with his management that the project would be done in five months. Now he would have to tell his management that he had been wrong. I told Ed that this shouldn't be a problem. After all, it was Julie who was paying for the system, and she understood why the estimate had increased from five to seven months. Also, for all we knew, the Team might finish in less than five months—or more than five months. At this point, we couldn't be certain. We would know a little better by the end of the first Sprint; at that point, we would have an idea of how quickly the Team could turn Product Backlog into functionality, and we could adjust the estimated number of

Sprints. Alternatively, if we wanted to increase the speed at which the Team was working, we could bring some people who knew the old cash system on board. These were all possibilities that Julie, the Team, and Ed could consider at the end of each Sprint.

Ed was profoundly uncomfortable with this approach. In the past, he'd always stuck to his initial estimates, and the Team had never let him down. Yes, he agreed, he now had better information about the project than he had before. However, the culture at MegaBank was such that once you said five months, that was all anyone remembered. Ed then turned to the Team and said, "Look, I know we have better information now, but even now it is still an estimate. We have five months, you've never let me down before, and I'm going to count on you not to let me down now."

A profound silence followed Ed's declaration. One team member later told me that it had sounded to him as though Ed were saying that it was business as usual, Scrum or no Scrum. They might be doing iterative, incremental development, but they were still going to cut corners whenever necessary. Ed was unwilling to tell his managers that software development is complex and that any estimate is just that—an estimate. Instead, the culture of believing that one can predict the future and that there is never a need to adjust predictions would continue to prevail at MegaBank. What the planning meeting had exposed was that until now the Team had been cutting corners to prop up this facade. Julie had heard Ed tell the Team that the date was more important than the quality, and that they should do whatever was needed to meet the date, even though Julie had asked for a quality product.

Lessons Learned

Scrum is easy to implement. The cash project began with the two-day Sprint planning meeting described earlier. However, Scrum requires a company to undergo a lot of organizational change to derive all of Scrum's benefits. In the cash project at MegaBank, we faced a management culture that viewed a preliminary estimate as a contract. Ed was unwilling to take on this misconception at this point in time, but Scrum would provide him, Tom, Julie, and the Team with more opportunities to do so. Every Sprint review meeting makes visible the difference between estimates and reality and between what the Team thought it could do and what it really did. At every such point, management has a chance to develop and moderate its expectations.

We had estimated the cost of increasing the quality of the functionality from "business as usual" to tested, clean, refactored code. We had an estimated cost for building a system that was more sustainable and maintainable. What we didn't have was a quantification of the sustainability and maintainability. When

Ed directed the Team to reduce the quality to increase speed, what was the cost to the organization? How did this cost compare to that of building in the quality? This information might have led Ed to revise his commitment to his managers.

Very few projects are so quantitative that it's possible to make objective decisions. At the end of every Sprint, the Product Owner is responsible for directing the Team to do work that is of the highest value to the organization. This work not only consists of turning the highest priority Product Backlog into functionality, but also consists of the adhering to engineering practices and standards. The work has two dimensions: the size of the work and the quality of the work. In the next example, we'll examine a project that contains the quantitative data needed to make the best possible decisions at the end of every Sprint. The example is a case study used during Certified ScrumMaster training classes.

Certified ScrumMasters Take on Return on Investment (ROI)

I hold certification sessions to train people who are familiar with and have used Scrum to be more effective as ScrumMasters. We look at how these people can better fulfill the role of ScrumMaster in their organizations so that their organizations can maximize the benefits they derive from Scrum. At the end of each certification session, everyone receives Scrum software and methodology to support their work as ScrumMaster. They are also inducted into the ScrumAlliance (*www.scrumalliance.org*), an alliance of Certified ScrumMasters.

The certification session employs team exercises based on a case study to drive home the meaning of Scrum's practices. The case study involves the hypothetical launch of a Major League Baseball (MLB) Web site. The case study is presented in the following sections. One of the exercises tests the Team members to see whether they are able to engage in meaningful dialog with a really tough customer: George Steinbrenner. The exercise asks the Team members to talk with Steinbrenner about some tough choices. Typical Team performances are presented at the end of the case study.

MLBTix

Overall attendance at baseball games has increased over the last 10 years. In some cities, such as Boston, almost all games are sold out, and obtaining tickets through normal channels is nearly impossible. MLB rules prohibit the resale of tickets at a profit. Scalping is illegal and has been cracked down on recently. The primary distribution channel for buying tickets is an online auction site, xAuction. Although all auctions for tickets on xAuction are supposed to be capped at the retail price plus expenses, MLB has learned that, through a variety of workarounds, these tickets are being scalped for prices of up to 1000 percent of the retail price.

Project Plan

The MLB commissioner's office hired an external consulting organization, Denture, to plan a project to manage the resale of baseball tickets. Denture delivered the final plan on November 15, and it was subsequently approved. Excerpts of the plan are provided here.

Project Background   New legislation mandates that as of the 2004 baseball season all ticket resales must take place through MLB-authorized facilities. MLB has decided to develop such a facility on the Web; the site will be known as MLBTix. Through functionality similar to the online auction site, xAuction, but specific to MLB, the public will be able to buy and sell MLB tickets online. Sellers will auction the tickets to the highest bidder, setting an initial bidding price of their own choice without floor or ceiling conditions established by MLBTix. The seller can also limit the duration of the auction by setting a start and an end date and time. If the ticket(s) are successfully sold, the buyer pays the seller through the MLBTix credit card facilities, and the seller mails the tickets to the buyer. Sellers will automatically be notified when buyers receive their tickets, at which point MLBTix will mail a check for the proceeds (less the 25 percent MLB fee) to the seller.

The commissioner will be announcing MLBTix at a news conference on January 15. He hopes to have some functionality available by opening day, March 30, 2004, and for the site to be fully functional by the All Star break, which begins July 18, 2004. Therefore, March 30, 2004 is the anticipated release date. On this date, the MLBTix site will be up, and buyers and sellers will be able to register. Sellers will be able to make tickets available at a fixed price, which buyers will be able to pay in full via credit card. MLBTix is a go-between, but all tickets are transferred directly from sellers to buyers. The release schedule mandates that on June 30, 2004, auction capability be added to site. Finally, on August 30, 2004, buyers will be able to buy groups of collocated tickets, view the locations of seats being sold, and check on inventory.

Funds for the project are ample and should not be considered an unreasonable constraint. The deliverables are the date and functionality. Facilities or packaged software to support MLBTix can be either bought or developed—whichever helps meet the date. The commissioner needs a heads-up on the likelihood that the MLBTix will be available by the above dates prior to his press conference.

Product Backlog   These are the functional requirements:

- Customers can register as potential sellers of tickets and be assigned a user ID and password.

- Customers can register as potential buyers of tickets and be assigned a user ID and password.

- Customers can maintain a profile under the user ID, including e-mail address, street address, preferences, and credit card information.

- Customers can place tickets up for auction, declaring a floor price, start of auction time/date, and end of auction time/date. Sufficient information should be provided so that buyers can ascertain that the tickets meet their requirements (for the right days, right teams, right number of seats located next to each other, and the seat locations in the ball park).

- Customers can cause an auction to be conducted for the tickets to registered buyers.

- Customer can have MLBTix successfully conclude the auction by awarding the tickets to the highest bidder by the end date and, at the same time, debiting the buyer's credit card and placing the funds in an MLBTix account.

- MLBTix will notify the seller of the successful sale of the tickets and provide the delivery information for the buyer.

- MLBTix will provide the buyer with a mechanism for indicating that the tickets were not successfully received by the selling date plus a specified period of time (for example, one week).

- MLBTix will transfer the funds for the ticket sale less 25 percent to the seller at the end of the specified delivery time, unless the buyer has indicated otherwise.

- MLBTix will transfer the 25 percent plus any interest to a corporate MLB account from the MLBTix account automatically.

- MLBTix will provide customers with inventory and inventory search capabilities for teams, tickets, dates, and seats.

- MLBTix will provide for promotions on MLBTix.

- MLBTix will be able to identify and ban abusers of MLBTix.

  These are nonfunctional requirements. MLBTix must be able to

- Handle 250,000 simultaneous users with sub-second response time.

- Be secure at the anticipated level of financial activity (2,000 tickets per day at an average selling price of $50).

- Be scalable to 1,000,000 simultaneous users if necessary.

- Be 99 percent available, 24 hours a day, 7 days a week.

This is the development context for bidders: The system will be created in a development environment for building Open Source products, using Intel technology and software running on an OpenSQL database server. The development Team members will all live within easy commuting distance of the development site. There are currently cubicles at the development site. The development environment is wireless and has all power and networking capabilities already operating. The development environment uses Open Source development tools such as Eclipse. The development Team is required to use a source code library, check in code every time it's changed, build the software at least daily, and unit and acceptance test the software every time that it is built. Scrum will be used as the development practice. Use of any other aspects of Extreme Programming or any other engineering practices, such as coding standards, is up to the Team. All of the developers on the Team must have excellent engineering skills and at least be familiar with Scrum and Extreme Programming. The Team must consist of development engineers with excellent design and coding skills. These engineers are responsible for all testing and user documentation, although they can hire contractors to assist with this. The engineers on the Team must average 10 years of progressive experience on software projects using complex technology and Open Source software products. All Team members must be baseball aficionados.

The Project

Imagine that after a quick request for proposal (RFP) process, the commissioner of MLB selected your organization to develop MLBTix. In your response to the RFP, you assured the commissioner that you can meet the release schedule. You were present with the commissioner at a press conference on January 15 when he announced MLBTix, and at this press conference, you demonstrated the functionality completed during the first Sprint. This Sprint began on December 7, 2003, and the Sprint review meeting was held on January 7, 2004.

Your Team has just completed its third Sprint, which ended on March 7, 2004. You have demonstrated the functionality developed during this Sprint to the commissioner. All the functionality necessary for the first release is in place. You intend to pull everything together into the production environment for the planned initiation of MLBTix on March 30, 2004, the start of the MLB 2004 season.

Uh-Oh!

At the Sprint planning meeting for the fourth Sprint, you and the Team become concerned about the capability of MLBTix to handle the kind of volumes that might be encountered. MLB has hired a public relations firm to market MLBTix, and it's done almost too good of a job: MLBTix has been the rage of every sports page and sports magazine. Everyone who knows about baseball knows about MLBTix and knows that it will be available as of 12:00 P.M. Eastern time on March 30, 2004. There are over 40 million baseball fans, and you know that almost no system could handle 40 million simultaneous hits.

You provide the commissioner with the following background information: The Team contacted several e-commerce retailers and determined that there would be on average 100 visits for every sale. The Team is unable to estimate the exact number of hits that will occur when the Web site first goes up but is worried that it will be more than it can handle. The MLB commissioner's research indicates that the site will likely sell 2,000 tickets per day in April 2004 and 5,000 per day thereafter for the rest of the season. The average price that will be charged by a seller above retail is $30, of which 25 percent will go to MLBTix. You have previously alerted the commissioner that the database technology Denture recommended the Team use is an iffy proposition at best, and scaling tests have shown the application to be database intensive. Even with all the tuning efforts from the consultants that have been brought in, and even running OpenSQL on the fastest RAID devices possible, the maximum number of simultaneous transactions that can be served with sub-three-second response time is 100 per second. Loads are expected to reach significant peaks at lunchtime and after dinner. The Team is concerned that peak volumes during normal production might overwhelm the server and that the knee of the performance curve will be very close to the 110-transactions-per-second rate. You have determined that the Miracle database will readily support the scaling requirements predicted by the commissioner, but it will take one more Sprint to trade out OpenSQL and implement Miracle database. The upshot? The application won't be ready until a month after the season opener.

What Advice Should You Provide?

You tell the commissioner all of this. You notice that the commissioner gets increasingly agitated during your presentation, tapping his feet, spitting at the floor, and uttering muffled expletives. He appears to be very unhappy. The commissioner tells you to knock off all of this technology mumbo-jumbo and tell him what he should do. He wants to know whether he should call in his public relations people and tell them to announce that he can't get MLBTix up. What should you advise the commissioner based on the above risk/reward model and your best instincts?

How the Teams Respond to This Exercise

I have used this exercise at more than 10 Certified ScrumMaster training courses, where people with some knowledge of Scrum and a lot of knowledge of systems development are trained to be ScrumMasters. I have asked over 200 of these people, grouped into 40 teams, to now provide advice to the commissioner. Here are some of their responses.

Team 1's Advice

Team 1 advises the commissioner that he has a scalability problem. Because of his aggressive MLBTix campaigning, the infrastructure will now have to handle more transactions than he had initially predicted. He had told them to use OpenSQL, which just doesn't scale to this sort of volume. As a result, Team 1 proposes to replace the OpenSQL database with the Miracle database, and this will take at least one additional month. Work will get started on it right away, and the commissioner will be informed as soon as possible whether it will take one or two months. In the meantime, Team 1 advises the commissioner to delay MLBTix indefinitely—at least until this problem is solved.

The commissioner responds, "I didn't understand a word you said until you told me that I'm going to be publicly humiliated. I told everyone that this site would be up on March 30, and now you're not only telling me that it won't be up then, but that you can't tell me for sure when it will be up. If Derek Jeter's agent tried this on me, I'd have him run up the flagpole."

Team 2's Advice

Team 2 advises the commissioner that he has nothing to worry about. They are really pleased that MLBTix has been such a success, and they are sure that the underlying technology recommended by Denture will work just fine. Otherwise, why would Denture have recommended it?

The commissioner's response: "I heard you reassure me, but I also heard you get ready to jump ship by blaming Denture if this doesn't work. I need advice, not weasel wording."

Team 3's Advice

Team 3 advises the commissioner that it will take steps to handle whatever number of fans come to MLBTix. Just as at Yankee Stadium, if there aren't enough ticket windows open, lines of fans will form. Team 3 will put in a facility that will tell the excess fans, "Due to overwhelming desire to buy tickets, you will be put on hold until the next agent is available." Then, every 30 seconds, the on-hold fan will be told, "Please stay in line. Your business is very important to us, and we want to serve you." Team 3 advises the commissioner that with this approach, MLBTix can service any number of customers without any additional cost.

The commissioner's response: "I really appreciate your not spending any additional money, but your frugality has really put me in a corner. I hate those recorded messages. I hate lines, but at least while I'm in a real line at

Yankee Stadium I can see what's happening. This is acceptable, but I'm not very pleased."

Team 4's Advice

Team 4 advises the commissioner that the success of the public relations campaign has made some additional work for the development team. It is risky to put up the site the way that it has been built so far—it might work, but its first few days might be atrocious. Team 4 would like to present him with some options. The first option is to let people start accessing MLBTix to register and see what will be at the site starting next week. Customers won't be able to buy and sell tickets until March 30, but the early availability might reduce the impact of the initial hit enough to avoid the problem. There is still a risk of trouble that you can't quantify, but this option won't carry any additional cost. The second option is to beef up the current capabilities by replicating the facilities for the teams with the highest anticipated volume: Yankees, Red Sox, Mariners, Braves, and Giants. This is similar to opening additional ticket windows. The cost of this option is $3.4 million dollars and will allow MLBTix to proceed on schedule with minimal risk. The third option is to delay the introduction of MLBTix by a month while upgrading all of the facilities to handle the greater than expected customer volume. The cost of this option is $1.1 million in additional cost and $425,000 in lost revenues to MLB from the 25 percent commission.

The Commissioner's response: "I understand. You have clearly laid out my alternatives so that it's easy for me to weigh my options. You spoke hardly a word of gobbledygook. Hmmm. Take an unknown risk of losing the whole thing, spend $3.4 million dollars and minimize my risk so that I can proceed as is, or pay $1.525 million and suffer the embarrassment of being late but manage to fix the problem for sure. We haven't evaluated how many customers we'll lose by being a month late, but that shouldn't be too much of an issue since we're a monopoly. Where else can the customers go? So I need to think about whether my pride is worth about $1.9 million dollars. Although I'm proud, I'm not dumb. Go with the third option!"

Lessons Learned

It was very hard for the teams to talk to the Product Owner—in this case, the commissioner—in a language that he could understand. Scrum is based on collaboration, but collaboration requires understanding, which in turn requires good communication. If the Product Owner speaks only in business terms and the Team speaks only in technical terms, there will be no communication, and thus no collaboration.

Think about the MegaBank cash project. When a manager suspected that the project would take longer than he had told his supervisors, he instructed the team to do whatever was necessary to make the date. If he'd had adequate data available, he could have instead weighed the cost of increasing the quality of the system during the additional two months vs. the cost of maintaining a weakly constructed and almost incomprehensible system over the course of its life. He ended up choosing to spend more on future maintenance, even though he didn't know what his choice would actually cost. As a team member commented to me, "Even though we're using Scrum, it's back to business as usual."

When Denture planned MLBTix, it provided enough information to enable the commissioner to make business tradeoffs. MLBTix was a complex project and was bound to hit snags. With the financial data in hand, however, various alternatives could be posited and a rational decision made. The commissioner priced his pride and chose to keep the money in his pocketbook. Plans that contain sufficient information make it easier to make rational decisions.

Of the four teams described here, only one used the financial data from the plan to offer options that the commissioner understood. The other teams either tried to discuss the problem in a language that wasn't meaningful to the commissioner or assumed the full risk of the situation by saying that everything was fine. Unfortunately, in most of the classes that I've held, many of the teams accept the risk and don't present options to the commissioner. This is a fairly typical response in the industry, where we in systems development hold the cards tightly to our chest until the end of the project and then let our customers find out for themselves how bad things really are. This isn't done purposefully; rather, it is the natural result of an environment in which developers don't really know where the project stands any better than management does.

Conclusions

Scrum provides many opportunities to inspect a project and make the necessary adaptations to optimize the benefits the project will secure for the organization. However, those responsible for making the adaptation must have adequate information if they are to make the best decisions. In the case of MegaBank, Julie and Ed didn't have enough information to decide whether to stick with a seven-month project schedule or to force a shorter schedule on the team in order to stick to the initial estimate of five months. In the absence of cost and benefit data, they went with prior commitments.

In distinct contrast, there was enough data to quantify the costs and benefits of the alternatives open to the MLB commissioner. Unfortunately, even in the presence of this data, very few teams take advantage of it. Most are so used to not having the data that they didn't even think to use it and ended up getting quite a tongue-lashing as a result.

As the MegaBank example showed, planning doesn't have to be extensive for a Scrum project to get going. However, it needs to be adequate enough to guide the inspection and adaptation cycle of empirical processes like Scrum. All projects could benefit from having the cost/benefit and assumptions data available to help guide these adaptations more meaningfully.

7

Project Reporting— Keeping Everything Visible

A Scrum project is controlled by means of frequent inspection of the project followed by necessary adaptations. Some of this information is communicated face-to-face. For instance, the Daily Scrum is open to everyone; attendees can quickly get a feel for the tone, attitude, and progress of a Sprint. The Sprint review meeting provides monthly insight into whether the project is creating valuable functionality, as well as the quality and capabilities of that functionality. Other information is communicated in writing. For instance, the Product Backlog details a project's requirements and lists them in order of priority. Everyone can evaluate the Product Backlog because it is stored in a public folder and its location is made known.

In addition to the dynamic information provided by written and visual information, formal reports are generated at the end of every Sprint. These reports provide a static snapshot of the project's progress. The reports are used to keep everyone with an interest in the project up-to-date on its progress. All of this information, both dynamic and static, is considered part of Scrum project reporting.

Let's look at how information about the status of Scrum projects has been put to use by several organizations. At MegaEnergy, management was uncomfortable with new ways of tracking project progress. We will see how the transition from traditional to Scrum project tracking was implemented. At MegaBank, the executive funding a project didn't like the periodic reports standard in Scrum. This executive wanted a summarized, graphical representation of the project's progress. We'll look at how this need was satisfied. At Service1st, the progress reported at the Daily Scrum by the team had been so summarized and abstracted that it was virtually meaningless. We'll look at why and how this happened and discuss ways to ensure that the amount of detail in reports is sufficient. It is not irrelevant that this same Service1st team also refused to update its Sprint Backlog. We'll look at the reasons for the team's refusal, the consequences of not updating the Sprint Backlog, and the way the situation was resolved.

New Project Reporting at the MegaEnergy Title Project

Scrum was brought into MegaEnergy through a pilot project, the Title project, which was referred to in Chapter 2. This project had already been attempted twice and had failed both times. An IT director had learned about Scrum and had convinced his fellow IT managers that they should try Scrum on the Title project. They all felt that this was an opportunity to assess Scrum. If Scrum could turn around the Title project, it would be deemed worthy of further evaluation.

Stakeholders are those who have a stake in a project's outcome, including those who funded the project and those who will be users of the system in development. Most projects at MegaEnergy offered project stakeholders only limited visibility into the project's operations and progress toward goals. These projects developed internal artifacts such as requirements statements, architectures, models, designs, and code. At the very end of the project, if the project hadn't stalled in developing these artifacts, they were all pulled together into a working system. Only then did the stakeholders get to see the actual system they were to use.

Project managers at MegaEnergy kept stakeholders and management apprised of a project's progress through periodic reports. Because traditional projects are managed at the task level, these reports documented the percentage of completed tasks, slippage in task completion, and any problems and recommended remedies. Since tasks have only a casual relationship to user functionality, these reports were often more frustrating than useful to stakeholders. A *Gantt report* was then used to track project progress. A Gantt report is a key tool in task-level project management, providing a visual mechanism for laying out all a project's work, the relationships between the work, and the resources assigned to the work.

MegaEnergy had a very formal and traditional project management process developed over the years by its program management office, staffed by senior people who had previously run pipeline construction projects. To them, the Gantt report was the Holy Grail for planning and controlling a project. Their solution to the first Title project failure had been to increase the extent of the initial planning and rigidly enforce change-control processes during the second attempt. They believed that the first project had failed because management had tolerated too many changes to the initial plan. When I heard this, I was reminded of Einstein's definition of insanity: doing the same thing over and over and expecting different results. Surprisingly, this approach is common. If a project being managed by a defined approach fails, people often assume that the project failed because the defined approach wasn't adhered to rigorously enough. They conclude that all that is needed for the project to succeed is increased control and project definition.

Senior management, including the steering committee for the Title project and the project management office, knew that something new was going to be tried on this third attempt at the Title project. The people staffing the program management office weren't familiar with empirical process control; Scrum was a big unknown to them. However, nobody objected to its use as long as the project was going to be controlled the way all projects at MegaEnergy were controlled—with Gantt reports.

This presented us with a dilemma. Should we provide Scrum training to senior management, including the people in the program management office? Should we make them aware of the radically different approach we were about to use on the Title project? Should we enter into a long discussion with them about the differences between defined and empirical process control? We knew that the discussion would have a large emotional impact. The people in the program management office had a long history of success at Mega-Energy. Their approach had been used to manage projects much larger than the Title project. Their take on the previous Title project failures was that it was a people failure, not a process failure. How could we convince them otherwise?

Scrum managers measure and track requirements, not tasks. The Product Backlog indicates the requirements, the prioritization of the requirements, and the anticipated grouping of the requirements into Sprints and releases. The Product Backlog at the start of a specific Sprint looks different from a Product Backlog at the start of a subsequent Sprint because business conditions might have caused the Product Backlog to change or be reprioritized. Some items in the Product Backlog might not have been completed during a Sprint and might have been reallocated to a future Sprint. The amount of Product Backlog initially planned for a release might include more or fewer requirements. The Product Owner might have restructured or repurposed the release. Planned Sprints might include more or fewer Product Backlog items than before as more is learned about the size of specific Product Backlog items, or as more is learned about the productivity of the teams working on the project.

Scrum reports represent a paradigm shift for most stakeholders and management. Traditionally, a plan is established and any variation from the plan is seen as undesirable. Periodic management reports are supposed to show how closely a project is to the initial plan. Scrum instead reports exceptions to the plan, responses to these exceptions, and the impact on the project plan. Scrum expects change and provides reports that track change and its impact on the project.

Solving the Problem

The ScrumMaster, Ruth, was a solid project manager at MegaEnergy. She knew MegaEnergy culture inside and out, and she knew the senior executives who would be receiving reports on the Title project's progress. She had worked with the people in the program management office and knew exactly what they wanted and why. She knew that Gantt reports were the core of their reporting system. She was skilled in preparing and managing these reports with Microsoft Project, the standard project management tool at MegaEnergy.

Ruth and I sat down to figure out how we could get the people in the program management office to permit us to proceed with Scrum. If we convinced them to let us try a new form of project management like Scrum, they wouldn't necessarily want it to succeed. They had a vested interest in the current method of project planning and management. Reporting would be tricky because we would have to justify every change. The words "empirical," "self-organizing," and "emergent" were virtually unknown in the program management office and would probably seem abhorrent to it.

The approach we settled on for introducing Scrum to senior management and the program management office reminds me of an old joke. John sees Hank pulling a long piece of rope up a narrow, winding mountain road. John asks Hank why he is doing this. Hank replies, "Because it's easier than pushing it!" The approach Ruth and I settled on wasn't as simple and straightforward as Scrum when it initially comes out of the can, but it seemed a lot simpler than trying to convince everyone that empirical process control, as embodied by Scrum, was a palatable alternative to their current approach. Ruth and I decided to provide management with the Gantt-based reports. However, rather than using task-based planning and reporting, we would plan and report requirements.

Our first step was to acquaint Ruth with Scrum's reports. Scrum defines four reports for the Product Owner and ScrumMaster to create at the end of each Sprint. The first lists the Product Backlog at the start of the previous Sprint. The second lists the Product Backlog at the start of the new Sprint. The third, the *Changes report*, details all of the differences between the Product Backlogs in the first two reports. The fourth report is the Product Backlog *Burndown report*.

The Changes report summarizes what happened during the Sprint, what was seen at the Sprint review, and what adaptations have been made to the project in response to the inspection at the Sprint review. Why have future Sprints been reformulated? Why was the release date or content reformulated? Why did the team complete fewer requirements than anticipated during the Sprint? Where was the incomplete work reprioritized in the Product Backlog? Why was the team less or more productive than it had anticipated? All of these questions are answered in the Changes report. The old and new Product Backlog reports are snapshots of the project between two Sprints. The Changes report documents these differences and their causes. A collection of Changes reports over a period of time documents the changes, inspections, and adaptations made during that period of time.

We then set about translating the Product Backlog into a Gantt report. The Product Backlog, shown in Figure 7-1, was maintained in a spreadsheet as a simple prioritized list of requirements. Dependencies between requirements are resolved by placing dependent requirements at a position in the list lower than the requirements on which they depend. Requirements are segmented into Sprints and released by unique rows in the list.

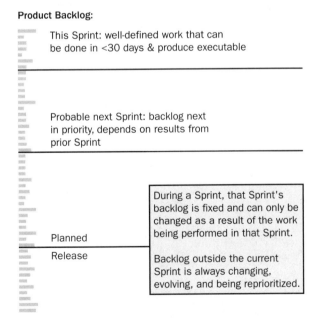

Product Backlog:

This Sprint: well-defined work that can be done in <30 days & produce executable

Probable next Sprint: backlog next in priority, depends on results from prior Sprint

During a Sprint, that Sprint's backlog is fixed and can only be changed as a result of the work being performed in that Sprint.

Backlog outside the current Sprint is always changing, evolving, and being reprioritized.

Planned

Release

Figure 7-1   Product Backlog example

A Gantt report is a lot more impressive than a Product Backlog list, as you can see in Figure 7-2. It is graphic, indicates dependencies with lines, comes in multiple colors, and is much more complicated than a simple list. But appearances can be deceiving. If a Gantt report includes only requirements, and not tasks, it is merely a graphical representation of the Product Backlog.

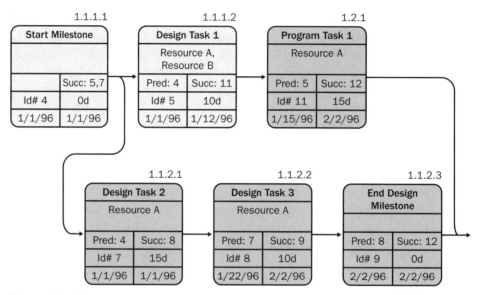

Figure 7-2   Gantt report example

Ruth opened the Title project Product Backlog spreadsheet in Microsoft Excel and opened a new project in Microsoft Project. She copied and pasted the entire Product Backlog list from Excel into Microsoft Project in the Task Name column. She then copied the estimates into the Duration column. She then arranged the requirements (Microsoft Project thought of them as *tasks*) by Sprint, as shown in Figure 7-3.

This transfer between two Microsoft products was straightforward. Ruth then populated the Work and Tracking views of the Microsoft Project views with the estimated work for each Product Backlog item, along with the start date and end date of each item's actual or planned Sprint. The percentage completed fields were normally 100 percent at the end of the Sprint. We decided that when they weren't, she would split the items and reallocate the undone work to future Sprints.

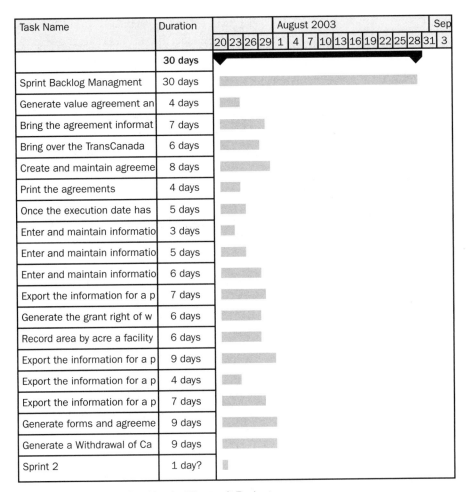

Task Name	Duration	August 2003												Sep
		20 23 26 29	1	4	7	10 13 16 19 22 25 28	31	3
	30 days							
Sprint Backlog Managment	30 days							
Generate value agreement an	4 days							
Bring the agreement informat	7 days							
Bring over the TransCanada	6 days							
Create and maintain agreeme	8 days							
Print the agreements	4 days							
Once the execution date has	5 days							
Enter and maintain informatio	3 days							
Enter and maintain informatio	5 days							
Enter and maintain informatio	6 days							
Export the information for a p	7 days							
Generate the grant right of w	6 days							
Record area by acre a facility	6 days							
Export the information for a p	9 days							
Export the information for a p	4 days							
Export the information for a p	7 days							
Generate forms and agreeme	9 days							
Generate a Withdrawal of Ca	9 days							
Sprint 2	1 day?							

Figure 7-3   Product Backlog in Microsoft Project

The only report that we couldn't readily translate to existing MegaEnergy reports was the Product Backlog Burndown report, shown in Figure 7-4. The Burndown report graphs remaining estimated workload over the course of the project. Workload at the start of each Sprint is measured by summing all open Product Backlog work estimates. From Sprint to Sprint, the increase or decrease in these sums can be used to assess progress toward completing all work for a release by an expected date.

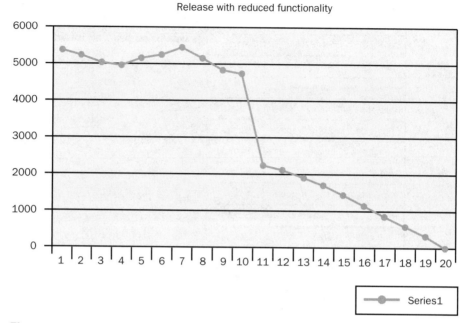

Figure 7-4   Product Backlog Burndown report

This Burndown report measures the amount of remaining Product Backlog work on the vertical axis and the time scale, by Sprint, on the horizontal axis. The Product Owner plots remaining quantity of Product Backlog work at the start of each Sprint. By drawing a line connecting the plots from all completed Sprints, a trend line indicating progress in completing all work can be drawn. By figuring out the average slope over the last several Sprints and drawing a trend line from the plots of these Sprints, the time when zero work remains can be determined, occurring when the trend line intersects the horizontal axis. Ruth and I decided that this was an important report. It would graphically present to management how the factors of functionality and time were interrelated. We decided to include it in the reports, but as an appendix.

When management got its reports at the end of the first Sprint, the new reports looked a lot like the old reports except that, as Ruth noted in the preface to the reports, she was tracking progress and completion of functionality rather than tasks. When Ruth went over these reports with the steering committee, she used the Product Backlog Burndown report to show the implications of completed Product Backlog to the entire release schedule. She then used the Product Backlogs to show the difference between the Product Backlog plans at the start of the Sprint and the end of the Sprint. In this case, the difference was fairly dramatic. The Product Owner had capitalized on the value of the first increment by choosing to implement it, meaning that the functionality in the increment was made production ready, the users in the Title department were trained, and the users started using this functionality in their everyday work. This decision introduced a release Sprint of two weeks into the Product Backlog, changing everything. As the steering committee discussed this, it came to realize a core benefit of Scrum: each Sprint's increment can potentially be implemented. In this case, the Product Owner felt that an early implementation was justified. The Product Owner inspected and adapted. The steering committee was exposed to the incremental nature of Scrum and the benefits of frequent inspection and adaptation.

Lessons Learned

Ruth correctly assumed that senior management didn't want to talk about process; it wanted to talk only about results. Introducing a new format for reporting project progress would require teaching management about Scrum. It would require getting the program management office to consider a whole new approach to managing projects. Senior management didn't care about Scrum. It cared about its investment in the project.

Ruth could have continued task-based reporting to senior management. If she had chosen to do so, she would have developed an anticipated task plan and fit each Sprint Backlog into it. She didn't have the time or inclination to do this, but she didn't want to change the reporting format. She correctly assessed that she could deliver a new message using the same reporting format, reporting progress on requirements and functionality rather than tasks. By fitting the Product Backlog into Microsoft Project, she was able to normalize the Product Backlog into a known format.

Translating Product Backlog to the Gantt report wasn't a very big effort. Ruth felt that it was certainly a much smaller effort than convincing the program management office that Scrum and Scrum reporting were acceptable. The only report that didn't readily fit was the Product Backlog Burndown report, which became an appendix to regular management reports. As management asked questions about the regular reports, Ruth was able to support her discussion with the Product Backlog Burndown reports. When management wanted to know the impact of the early release, Ruth was able to show it to management on the Burndown reports. Ruth was able to teach management how to manage a Scrum project without having to teach it a whole new vocabulary.

Scrum proves its value as projects succeed. However, it is a radically different approach from traditional project management, expecting change rather than fearing it. Adaptation is a normal part of the project rather than an exception. If these concepts are theoretically discussed, most people agree on the reasonableness of the approach. When these concepts are brought up in the context of a critical project, however, management is often extremely wary. Managers want to know why this approach is being suggested. They ask if the approach is risky, and whether allowing this much change isn't inviting disaster. In this case, Ruth showed the value of the new approach by putting her mouth where management's money was. She showed the benefits and value of Scrum to management without its knowing or caring about the concepts or theory of agile processes. All management knew was that something good was afoot. As the CEO of another company stated at a Sprint review, "I don't know what this Scrum is, but I like it." That's the way it should be.

Getting More Information at MegaBank

MegaBank was introduced in earlier chapters. The MegaBank Information Technology (MBIT) organization manages all MegaBank operations, technologies, and infrastructure. The individual banks develop the software for themselves and their clients and are collectively required to follow the decisions and use the operations of MBIT.

MBIT is the technology brain trust for MegaBank. Advanced technologies such as biometrics are researched and progressively rolled out under its auspices. Since the late 1990s, MBIT had used a Web site, MBITWeb, to store, post, and host discussion groups as new technologies were investigated. MBITWeb wasn't user-friendly and had been the subject of many complaints. Its usage was also rather low. To address these problems, MBIT funded an upgrade project. Developers from one of the banks and MBIT technologists jointly composed the team. Scrum was selected as the development process. The individual banks had successfully used Scrum, and MBIT wanted to see what it was all about. Tom, a MegaBank employee who had previously used Scrum, was made ScrumMaster. Andy, an MBIT manager, was the Product Owner. Both Tom and Andy were team members as well.

MBIT management had learned to live with task-based reporting. It had devised other ways of learning what was really going on. Sometimes it asked for demonstrations. Sometimes it called for project reviews, at which it grilled the team. Scrum posed a problem for these executives. The ScrumMaster protects the Team from predations during the Sprint. The ploys management had traditionally resorted to aren't allowed in Scrum. When Scrum is first implemented, sometimes this frustrates management, and this frustration boils over until a mechanism for satisfying it is devised. In the worst cases, management withdraws and says that Scrum has cut it out of the loop. Jim, the MBIT vice president who had funded the MBITWeb project and the Product Owner's manager, had tried such a predation, asking for a demonstration in the middle of the Sprint. He boiled over when Tom and Andy told him to wait until the Sprint review meeting at the end of the Sprint.

Jim demanded a meeting with Helen, the IT director of the bank supporting the project. Jim was acerbic by nature, initially putting people on the defensive rather than collaborating with them to get information and work out solutions. He demanded that Helen tell him what sort of strange process Scrum was if it required that all progress be hidden for 30 days. He didn't have time to attend Daily Scrums, so how was he to know if things were OK? Tom and Andy had shown him the Scrum reports, but they were meaningless to him. This was a deep technology project, employing a number of advanced IBM technologies. How could he know whether these technologies were working effectively? How could he know to what degree the different parts of MBITWeb were developed every Sprint? How, how, how? By the time Helen left Jim's office, she felt as though a hurricane had just passed through her!

Solving the Problem

Helen regrouped with Tom and Andy and told them that Jim was dissatisfied with the current reports. They simply did not satisfy his technical curiosity about the details of the development. Furthermore, Jim worked in an intellectually aggressive organization: at MBIT, anyone could question you about your projects, so you were expected to have the details at your fingertips at all times. If Jim didn't understand what was going on in his project, he would wind up looking bad.

Helen, Jim, and Andy understood that Jim was different from the usual project stakeholder. The user functionality was only a small part of what he cared about. He also cared about the technologies being explored by the project. His boss was more likely to question him about portlet technology than user functionality. Jim required reports containing information about both. Because Jim was busy and impatient, these reports would have to be easy for him to grasp, assimilate, and use to track project progress.

Helen, Jim, and Andy presented the problem to the team. Together, they devised a management view of the project's technology architecture, as shown in Figure 7-5. This view was simply a cleaned-up version of the system architecture diagrammed on the wall of the team room. They divided the technology into layers of services: presentation, application, and data. The team then assigned colors to the milestones for this project. The milestones were simply arbitrary dates when management wanted certain product capabilities. These were later synchronized with Sprint review dates. Blue represented the first milestone. When the services were partially completed, they were colored light blue. When they were completed, they were colored dark blue. The same progression was devised for the second milestone, with green representing progress, and so on. As the team began working on a service, they used the light shade of a color. When they had finished with a service, they changed the light shade of the color to the darker shade of the color.

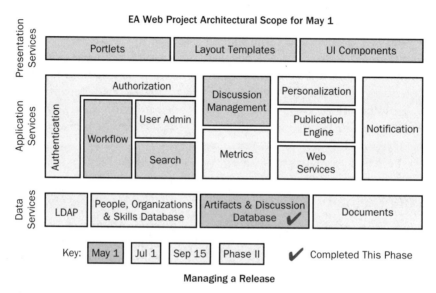

Figure 7-5   Technology progress report

The technology progress report was posted on the door of the team room, where it was visible to anyone walking by. A copy was delivered to Jim weekly, keeping him up-to-date on progress more frequently than once a month. When Jim met members of the MBITWeb team in the hallways and asked about progress, the conversation was held in terms of the services and service names on the technology progress report.

At the Sprint reviews, the team started by discussing the progress made on the various services. When the team demonstrated a transaction that threaded services together, from presentation through application to data services and back, it showed the progress of the transaction on the technology report.

Lessons Learned

After several Sprints, most managers are more than satisfied with the visibility Scrum provides them into the project and its progress. The trick is how to get over these first few Sprints. My customers and I have had to devise any number of ancillary reporting mechanisms to Scrum to do so. This could potentially be viewed as a weakness of Scrum. But keep in mind that Scrum represents a major shift in thinking and acting, and many people don't really understand Scrum until they have experienced it. In the meantime, these interim reports bridge the gap between when the first Sprint starts and when management feels comfortable with the visibility it has into the project through Sprint reviews and Scrum reports.

During the transition to Scrum, these ancillary and customized reports are necessary. You don't want Scrum rules to be broken and the team to be disrupted. On the other hand, you don't want management to withdraw or boil over. As ScrumMaster, your job is the Scrum process and its adoption by the organization. You are responsible for figuring out and delivering these interim-reporting mechanisms whenever they are needed.

Not Everything Is Visible at Service1st

Once again, we visit Service1st for instruction in Scrum. Scrum was being used to develop release 9.0 of Service1st's customer service software. The team committed to developing a lot of functionality in its very first Sprint. Irene, the ScrumMaster, tried to get the team to tone down its commitment, but the team insisted that it could complete all of the Product Backlog that it had selected. At the Sprint review, the team successfully demonstrated all of the functionality as well as several additional features. Management was ecstatic: Scrum was wonderful; the team was wonderful; everything was wonderful. Management thought that releases could now occur more frequently or contain more functionality.

But I was suspicious. During the demonstration, the team members had followed a scripted demonstration and had seemed reluctant to stray from the script. The reason was probably that they were operating under time constraints, but what if this wasn't the case? In wartime, safe paths through minefields are marked with white lines. If you stay within the white lines, you are OK. If you wander outside the white lines, no one knows what might happen! The demonstration had seemed to be scripted to operate within white lines. I stayed after the Sprint review with several team members and exercised the functionality myself. The system encountered various errors, stack overflows, traces, and severe crashes whenever I departed from the script, straying outside the white lines.

Upon closer inspection, the team's apparent high productivity was found to be the result of not having tested the functionality and not fixing bugs found during the testing. The team was so excited about presenting that it forgot Scrum's rule of sashimi: Every increment of potentially shippable product functionality that is demonstrated at the Sprint review must be complete. It must contain all analysis, design, coding, testing, documentation, and anything else appropriate for the application—a complete slice of the product.

I suggested to Irene that she not let the team proceed with any new functionality until it had really completed the functionality it had already demonstrated. Incomplete testing and bug fixing should be put on the Product Backlog as uncompleted work. The code was fresh in the team's mind; debugging it in the next Sprint would take less time now than it would later. Making the team debug the code immediately would also reinforce the message that only completed work was acceptable. But the team rebelled. It feared that the next Sprint review would be humiliating. In the first Sprint review, it had come off as SuperTeam. In the next Sprint review, it would look like Elmer Fudd with nothing new to demonstrate. How could it demonstrate the same functionality as the prior Sprint review, adding only that the functionality now worked?

Scrum can't be learned overnight. The team hadn't realized the implications of the rule of sashimi: that every increment must consist of potentially shippable functionality, completely tested and documented. Now it understood this. But should the team be punished for its ignorance? Should the team have to look incompetent in front of management? Irene wisely relented, but only a little bit. After some scheming, the team and Product Owner decided that the team would also build a piece of workflow functionality that would show the previously demonstrated functionality working together. Although this wasn't much additional work, the demonstration of it would save the team's pride. After all, the team had done a lot of work.

The team came to the first Daily Scrum of the new Sprint. In sequence, the team members reported that they were either testing or fixing bugs. The meeting was complete in five minutes, but no useful information had been exchanged. Of course they were working on bugs. But which bugs were they working on? Without each team member clearly identifying what he or she was working on, the Daily Scrum was useless. No real commitments were being made and checked on. Nobody knew the areas of code their teammates were looking at, so they could not offer advice or help. Basically, the team members had reported that they had worked yesterday and were planning on working more today.

The Reality

The team had overachieved on coding by underachieving on testing. It had hacked together a demonstration that worked only in the lab and at the presentation. The functionality certainly wasn't sashimi. If the Product Owner had called for the code's release after the Sprint review, a lot more work would be required before everything was nailed down. In traditional projects, the team spends months analyzing and designing without producing anything of interest to stakeholders. The Service1st team had done the reverse, demonstrating more functionality than had been completed. The stakeholders now believed that they were further along than they really were. They were excited about a situation that didn't really exist!

The Agile Manifesto is a statement of values and principles that describe the various agile processes, of which Scrum is one. The Agile Manifesto was developed in February 2001; more information is available at *www.agilealliance.org*. In the Agile Manifesto, the seventh of twelve principles is, "Working software is the primary measure of progress." When a stakeholder or the Product Owner sees a piece of functionality demonstrated, he or she can assume that it is complete. The Product Owner bases his or her view of progress on this belief. When any increment is not complete, all incomplete work must be identified and restored to the Product Backlog as incomplete work.

Irene was a freshly baked ScrumMaster, having received her certification just the previous month. As such, it was understandable that she had overlooked a key symptom of trouble. The team had refused to keep the Sprint Backlog up-to-date throughout the project. After the Sprint planning meeting, the Sprint Backlog went untouched. When a team is hacking together functionality, it often doesn't spend much time on analysis, design, and testing. It codes, codes, and then codes again. It then cobbles everything together with chewing gum for a demonstration. When the team is developing software coherently, it plans and allocates all of the work necessary to build a complete increment of functionality. The Sprint Backlog should reflect this attention to detail.

The next Sprint planning meeting took over a day. Irene wouldn't let the team proceed with the Sprint until it had a detailed Sprint Backlog. Irene watched while the team detailed the work needed to define the new workflow functionality. She then made the team commit to updating the Sprint Backlog every day before leaving work.

You would think that the team would have learned everything there is to know about self-management from the first Sprint. But the excitement of Scrum can lead to overlooking the hard parts of it. Managing yourself is hard; it's much easier, although less satisfying, to let someone else manage you. The Sprint Backlog that the team developed during the Sprint planning meeting consisted of two types of work. For each piece of functionality demonstrated in the previous Sprint, there was an entry to test it and then fix any bugs that were found. The tasks to build the new workflow functionality composed the rest of the Sprint Backlog. This work was laid out and then reported on in detail. However, the test and debug tasks were abstracted and summarized to such an extent that the number of hours remaining couldn't be determined. Was the Sprint behind or ahead of schedule? Nobody knew. The test and debug work never burned down because the amount of work remaining was unknown.

Irene met with the team and described the trouble she had inspecting its progress. She told the team that Scrum works only when everything is visible and everyone can inspect progress and recommend adaptations. The team members were reporting that they were testing for and fixing bugs, but the information they provided wasn't detailed enough to be useful. When one team member reported on his or her work, the other team members didn't know whether they should help. They couldn't assess whether they were working on a similar problem or were even in the same area of functionality or code. The number of bugs detected and fixed couldn't be ascertained.

Irene asked that the team members report by the specific test employed and the specific bugs found. She asked that a test be identified for every aspect of functionality previously coded. These tests should then be entered into the Sprint Backlog. She also asked the team to create testing and bug metrics. She wanted the team to know the number of tests employed, bugs uncovered, and bugs fixed, and she wanted the team to understand how many bugs would remain unfixed at the end of the Sprint. She wanted the team to know the quality of the product that it was building. She was teaching a team that previously had counted on a quality assurance (QA) group to test the product to instead take on this responsibility itself.

Prior to the next Daily Scrum, Irene posted the Sprint Backlog on the wall of the team room. When each team member reported on his or her specific tests and bugs, Irene checked that they were listed on the Sprint Backlog. She did this at every Daily Scrum going forward, ensuring that the team managed its work at the level of specificity necessary to know what was going on. The team and Irene were able to monitor the bug trends. Was the bug count going up or down? Were any new bugs being introduced as old ones were being fixed?

Reporting at the Daily Scrum has to be specific. Commitments are real only if they can be assessed. In the absence of specificity, Irene's team was hiding behind the umbrella phrase of "bug-fixing." The team members couldn't plan or synchronize their work.

Lessons Learned

The team was excited about no longer being under the constraints of someone else's plan. It was excited about being able to get to the coding. It was excited about the opportunity to prove how much it could do. In sum, all of this excitement led the team to forget solid engineering practices.

Irene taught the team how to manage itself. It had to understand all aspects of what it was doing and frequently correlate its activities in order to deliver a completed set of functionality. Self-organizing teams aren't unmanaged teams. To manage itself, a team must have a plan and report against that plan. The details of the plan and the reporting must be specific enough to be meaningful. The team has to be able to synchronize its work.

A Scrum team is self-organizing. It assumes responsibility for planning its own work. The Sprint Backlog is the visible manifestation of the team fulfilling this responsibility. I've seen teams of three very skilled engineers not use a Sprint Backlog, delivering solid functionality from plans they kept in their heads. However, most teams need to think through what they are doing and write it down so that team members can refer back to a plan as they work. The Daily Scrum synchronizes everyone's work only if the work has been thought through. Otherwise, the Daily Scrum is useless.

The ScrumMaster has to teach, enforce, and reinforce the rule of sashimi. Sometimes teams try to cut corners. Sometimes teams are so used to waterfall development processes that they view testing as someone else's problem. The mechanism for detecting whether the team is doing all necessary work is the Sprint Backlog. The ScrumMaster ensures that testing activities are also separately delineated in the Sprint Backlog until the team understands the meaning of the word "complete." Once the team understands that the process of developing functionality includes analysis, design, coding, testing, and documentation, all of these unique waterfall activities can be collapsed into one Sprint Backlog task.

Conclusions

Scrum works only if everything is kept visible for frequent inspection and adaptation. To be empirical, everyone must know that about which they are inspecting. Practices such as the Sprint review meeting, the Daily Scrum, the Sprint Backlog, and the Product Backlog keep everything visible for inspection. Rules such as not being able to interrupt a team during a Sprint keep the adaptations from turning meaningful progress into floundering, as overadaptation overwhelms the project.

The ScrumMaster must keep everything visible at a meaningful level of detail. At MegaEnergy, Scrum was made visible through existing reporting mechanisms. Ruth made learning about Scrum easy for executives because she used their language. At MegaBank, Helen had the team figure out Jim's language. Only then was Jim able to understand a Scrum project's progress. To create visibility in these instances, the ScrumMaster had to adapt Scrum to the organization.

In the Service1st example, at first the team didn't maintain the Sprint Backlog, obscuring their lack of planning. Then the team didn't put enough detail into the Sprint Backlog, obscuring its lack of progress in testing and bug fixing and undermining the value of Daily Scrums. To create visibility, the ScrumMaster had to teach the team the importance of the Sprint Backlog practices to self-organization. The Sprint Backlog is the team's Sprint plan.

A ScrumMaster must be vigilant. If the ScrumMaster is unclear about what's going on, so is everyone else. Make sure everything is visible. Find a way to make Scrum understandable to everyone in his or her vocabulary. Some people want to understand Scrum and will track a projects' progress in Scrum terms. Other people want to understand the project only in the traditional context. Adapting Scrum to their vocabulary eases the change from traditional processes to the Scrum process.

8

The Team

Scrum's productivity stems from doing the right things first and doing those things very effectively. The Product Owner queues up the right work by prioritizing the Product Backlog. How does the Team maximize its productivity, though? Assuming that lines of code per day or function points per person-month are good productivity measurements, who tells the Team how to maximize them? In Scrum, the Team figures out how to maximize its productivity itself; the job of planning and executing the work belongs solely to the Team. The ScrumMaster and others can guide, advise, and inform the Team, but it is the Team's responsibility to manage itself.

At the heart of the solution is the Team working without interruption for the 30-day Sprint. Having selected the Product Backlog for a Sprint, the Team has mutually committed to turning it into an increment of potentially shippable product increment in 30 calendar days. Once the Team makes this commitment, the clock starts ticking. The Sprint is a time-box within which the Team does whatever is necessary to meet its commitment. At the end of the Sprint, the Team demonstrates the working functionality to the Product Owner.

As organizations implement Scrum, epiphanies are experienced, moments when people say, "Aha! Now I get it." One such epiphany is when a Team realizes that it manages itself. The first glimpse comes during the Sprint planning meeting. The Team has selected the Product Backlog for the next Sprint—what now? The silence lengthens as the Team waits for someone to tell it what to do. The discomfort grows; when will someone step in and describe the work to the Team? At this point, I remind the Team that the Sprint has started, that there are now only 29.98 days left before the Sprint review meeting, and that no one is going to tell it what to do; the Team has to figure out its work itself. After a few more minutes, a team member speaks up, "Why don't we figure out what the portlets should look like?" Another team member chimes in, "Do we have any standards for portlet look and feel?"

The Team is now on its way. It has started to manage itself, to realize that only it can figure out the best way to reduce the Product Backlog to the demonstrable functionality.

The transition from a Team that is managed to a Team that manages itself is difficult, but the payback in productivity and pleasure of work is impressive. The ScrumMaster's job is to lead the Team through this transition. The ScrumMaster coaches the Team to use the inspection and adaptation of the Daily Scrum to guide itself, the visibility aspects of Scrum to guide the required quality of its work, and the Sprint retrospective meeting to reflect and adapt again and again. The purpose of the Sprint retrospective is to inspect how the Scrum process worked during the last Sprint and adjust it to improve the next Sprint. These meetings are time-boxed at two hours.

In this chapter, we'll look at an organization, Service1st, going through this difficult transition. We'll look at teams struggling to learn self-organization and self-management. We'll see how hard it is for ScrumMasters and their teams to start organizing and managing themselves. Self-organization and self-management are easy to grasp on an intellectual level, but they often prove difficult to implement. Such concepts are counterintuitive to the culture of many workplaces, and many teams veer off track. Then we'll take a look at me going over the top at WebNewSite, so that you can reflect on what represents reasonable or unreasonable leadership from a ScrumMaster.

Team Formation at Service1st

As an organization transitions to Scrum, the Team bears the brunt of the change. Whereas before the project manager told the Team what to do, now the Team has to figure out what to do on its own. In the past, team members worked on their own, but now they work with each other. Before Scrum, team members had lots of time to complete a release, but now they are asked to pull together potentially releasable software at the end of each Sprint. We've looked at several instances of Service1st using Scrum in previous chapters. In this chapter, we'll see the trials and tribulations the team went through as Service1st learned the ins and outs of Scrum.

One hundred and twenty people worked in the development organization. Service1st used a sequential, or waterfall, life cycle, and the staff was organized accordingly, with designers reporting to a design manager, coders reporting to a programming manager, testers reporting to a quality assurance (QA) manager, and writers reporting to a documentation manager. Service1st releases a new version of its software approximately every six months. When I arrived to implement Scrum, the next planned release involved an aggressive integration into Service1st's main product line of workflow and collaboration software built by a new partner.

The vice president of development, Hal, was dissatisfied with the waterfall process; he was particularly displeased by the crunch that happened during the last two months of every release cycle. It appeared to him that his development organization thought about the work for four months, eventually felt the pressure of the nearing release date, and then worked days, nights, and weekends to code, test, and document. The result was an exhausted staff in no shape for the next release cycle.

After extensive investigation by Hal and his managers, Hal decided to try Scrum. Scrum's iterative, incremental practices would provide regular progress throughout the release cycle. I met with Hal and his managers to discuss how to get started: define the Product Backlog for the release, divide the development organization into cross-functional Scrum teams, and parse the work among the teams. We struggled with this task, trying very hard to take into account team dynamics, personalities, domain knowledge, and couplings between functionalities. We wanted the teams to get along as well as possible, have all of the knowledge and skills needed to do the assigned work, and not be dependent on the progress of other teams for their own team's success. We weren't able to do this to our satisfaction without splitting people with key domain or technical knowledge between teams. One individual, for example, was assigned to four different teams. Although this was hardly ideal, we didn't want to spend the entire six months planning for the release, either, so we decided to move on.

I discussed with Hal and his managers some of the most important things that can be done to optimize team performance. I recommended removing the cubicles and setting up collocated team spaces. Hal decided to wait on this recommendation because they had recently built the cubicles. I also recommended eliminating all of the development artifacts—like design documents—that existed only to support the waterfall approach. Scrum relies on high-bandwidth, face-to-face communication and teamwork; cubicles and unneeded artifacts promote isolation and misunderstandings.

I conducted a ScrumMaster training session to prepare Hal's managers for Scrum. During this training, I emphasized that ScrumMasters have no authority over the development teams; they are present only to ensure that the Scrum process is adhered to and that the teams' needs are met. We then kicked off the Scrum and the release for the teams with Sprint planning meetings. The teams started and ended their Sprints simultaneously to facilitate the overall review of the release's progress every 30 days. During these initial Sprint planning meetings, we reinforced the various Scrum rules. In particular, we emphasized that a Team is self-managing, that it has only 30 days to do its work, and that its work must result in completely developed pieces of functionality.

Some of the teams expressed doubts that the teams as constituted were adequate. Some teams didn't seem to have enough testers to do all of the testing or enough writers to create all of the documentation. In response, I explained to them that a Team is cross-functional: in situations where everyone is chipping in to build the functionality, you don't have to be a tester to test, or a designer to design.

Learning Who's the Boss: The Transition

The teams at Service1st met every day for the Daily Scrum. Alicia, the Scrum-Master of several of the teams, directed the meetings crisply and professionally, ensuring that everyone answered these three questions: What have you done since the last Daily Scrum? What are you planning on doing between now and the next Daily Scrum? Do you have any impediments to report? She helped the teams complete their meetings within the time-box of 15 minutes.

When Alicia went on vacation, another ScrumMaster, George, filled in for her. He was pleased at how crisply the Daily Scrums went, but nonetheless he was troubled by a strange feeling that something was amiss. After several days, he realized that he heard hardly any requests for help or offers of help. There were no side comments that he had to contain to keep the meeting to 15 minutes. After some sleuthing, George figured out why. As team members reported progress, they were looking at George instead of at other team members. They were doing so because they were reporting to George, who they saw as their project manager. Even though they'd been told otherwise, the team members still felt that George was in charge and thought that the Daily Scrum was a meeting at which they would report to him, and not a forum at which they'd synchronize with each other.

Once George realized this, he talked it over with the team members, reinforcing the message that he was there only to facilitate communication among team members. The meeting was for the team, and the team members should make a point of avoiding looking at him. To help the team members adjust to the real purpose of the Daily Scrum, George requested that the team members look at each other when reporting.

Lessons Learned

Being managed by someone else is totally ingrained in our life and work experience. Parents, teachers, and bosses who teach us to self-manage instead of striving to fulfill their expectations are rare. Why should we expect that when we tell a Team that it is responsible for managing itself, it will know what we are talking about? "Self-management" is just a phrase to them; it isn't yet something real. A Team requires concrete experience with Scrum before it can truly understand how to manage itself and how to take the responsibility and authority for planning and conducting its own activities. Not only must the ScrumMaster help the Team to acquire this experience, but the ScrumMaster must also do so while overcoming his or her own tendencies to manage the Team. Both the ScrumMaster and the Team have to learn anew how to approach the issue of management.

Learning to Engineer Better: The Transition

During a Daily Scrum, I heard one developer report that he needed another developer to check in some code so that he could make some modifications. The good news was that the Team was using a source code management system; the bad news was that there were apparently some bad engineering practices; otherwise, the code would be checked in regularly. I asked the team members if I could meet with them after the Daily Scrum.

When we got together, I went over the concept of an increment of potentially shippable product functionality. Each Sprint, the Team commits to turning selected Product Backlog into such an increment. For the functionality to be potentially shippable, it has to be clean. The team members wanted to know what I meant by "clean." Did I mean free from bugs? I answered in the affirmative and told them that clean code not only has to be free from bugs, but must also adhere to coding standards, have been refactored to remove any duplicate or ill-structured code, contain no clever programming tricks, and be easy to read and understand. Code has to be all of these things for it to be sustainable and maintainable. If code isn't clean in all of these respects, developing functionality in future Sprints will take more and more time. The code will become more turgid, unreadable, and difficult to debug. I also reminded the team members that Scrum requires transparency. When the Team demonstrates functionality to the Product Owner and stakeholders at the Sprint review, those viewing the functionality have a right to presume that the code is complete, meaning not only that the code is written but also that it is written according to standards, easy to read, refactored, unit tested, harness tested, and even functionality tested. If this isn't true, the Team isn't allowed to demonstrate the functionality, because in that case, the viewer's assumption would be incorrect.

This conversation provided the team with some background. The team members now wanted to know why I was concerned about the code not being checked in. I said that code is often checked at a higher rate than usual so as to facilitate frequent builds. A *build* is a compilation of all of the code in a system or subsystem to validate that all of the code can be pulled together into a clean set of machine-readable instructions. The build is usually followed by automated tests to ensure that all of the functionality works.

The team members looked at me innocently. They told me that, unless there were special circumstances, they built the system only toward the end of the development cycle. Now that they were using Scrum, they planned to start builds around the twenty-second or twenty-third day. Then they would start cleaning everything up. This revelation took me by surprise. Various team members were reporting during the Daily Scrum that certain functionalities were complete, but according to what I was hearing now, nothing had yet been checked back into the source code library, built, and tested. I asked whether this was the case, and a silence suddenly descended on the meeting. Everyone realized that there was a problem. One Team member, Jareesh, wanted to know how he could possibly check in code that frequently. He often kept code checked out for 5 or even 10 days while he was developing functionality. I asked how he could know on a given day that the code he had developed wasn't in conflict with someone else's code if he hadn't checked in his code. He said that if he checked it in frequently, he would have to make such adjustments daily, but that by checking in his code only when it was complete, he had to make such an adjustment only once.

I again reminded the Team that Scrum requires complete transparency. Every day, the team has to synchronize its work so that it knows where it stands. Otherwise, team members might make incorrect assumptions about the completeness and adequacy of their work. They might think that their code is fine, while Jareesh is working on code that negates or diminishes the value of their work. Scrum relies on empirical process control, which in turn is based on frequent inspections and adaptation. If the Team couldn't inspect its status at least daily, how could it adapt to unforeseen change? How could it know that such change had even occurred? How could the team avoid the traditional death march of pulling everything together at the end of a development cycle—in this case, a Sprint—if it didn't pull everything together at least daily?

I told the team members that I couldn't tell them how to develop software. I could question them about the completeness of their code, and I could suggest remedies, but the solution was their responsibility. I could help their ScrumMaster make sure that they were following the Scrum process, however. In this case, this meant that the team members had to devise engineering practices such that every day all of the code that had been written was checked in, built, and tested. Just as at the end of the Sprint, every day this code had to be clean—or else the inspection and adaptation mechanisms of Scrum wouldn't work.

Lessons Learned

From this experience, the Team learned about the way Scrum's inspect and adapt mechanisms necessarily impacted some of its practices. The Team had initially thought that the Daily Scrum was only a short meeting at which the

Team would synchronize its work and plan for the coming day. However, the subtle but important aspect of this synchronization is that it requires the Team to know exactly where it is and where it isn't. Without engineering practices that supported such an assertion, the Team would be unable to synchronize its work. The team members and I spent the next several weeks looking into the engineering practices that they might adopt. I helped team members understand the engineering environment and build processes that are necessary for Scrum to work. I also helped them understand several of the Extreme Programming practices—such as shared code, coding standards, and pair programming—that might help them meet this need.

Engineering excellence for its own sake is a hard sell because it is theoretical, and Teams have real work to do. Scrum, however, requires engineering excellence for its inspect and adapt practices to work. This organization couldn't realize all of Scrum's benefits without improving its engineering practices. By the end of the Sprint, the team members were on their way to improving their engineering practices and were working with other teams to ensure that they all had common practices. This task, of course, would never be complete, as improving engineering competence and professionalism is an unending process. However, they were on the right road, and their software, the company, and their careers would benefit from their efforts.

Learning to Self-Organize: The Transition

As happens in most organizations starting to use Scrum, many of Service1st's teams overcommitted themselves for the first Sprint. Rather than using the full time of the first Sprint planning meeting to detail all of the tasks required to build the functionality, the teams shortchanged the effort and went by gut feel. The team members selected Product Backlog that they felt they could reasonably convert to functionality within the Sprint's 30 days. But once the team members got to work, they found that there was more to do than had been anticipated. At the end of the first Sprint, these teams were able to demonstrate less than they had hoped; in once instance, a team demonstrated largely untested functionality. Their ScrumMaster later reminded them that this broke a Scrum rule and was not to happen again.

Having learned from their experience during the first Sprint, the teams spent much more time planning the second Sprint. They detailed the tasks, reviewed available hours, weighted availability against commitment, and—as a result—undercommitted. The teams had assigned each task more time than was necessary; this led the teams to overestimate the amount of work that would be required to develop the selected functionality. Halfway through the second Sprint, the teams realized that they had time and energy left over. Working with their Product Owners, they selected more top-priority requirements from the Product Backlog and tackled those as well. The second Sprint review was a rousing success. Not only had the teams built functionality, but management was also able to get a clear picture of what the release would look like early in the release cycle. Management was able to provide guidance as the release progressed, rather than waiting until the end of the release cycle.

After the second Sprint review, Hal held a Sprint retrospective meeting. We conducted this retrospective with the entire development organization, including all the teams and their members, with everyone sitting in a large circle. Going around the circle, the team members spoke about what they felt had worked and what needed improvement during the next Sprint. Hal acted as scribe, summarizing everyone's comments on a whiteboard. Each person identified what had gone right during the Sprint and what he or she would like to improve for the next Sprint.

What was the outcome of the Sprint retrospective? Many at Service1st were pleased to be helping each other; when someone fell behind, other team members jumped in and helped. Some of the coders were delighted to be sitting next to testers because they were able to understand the full set of tests that would later be applied even while they were still in the process of coding. Everyone was glad to be making evident progress on the release so early in the release cycle. One programmer was thrilled because he had gotten to talk to and work with a designer with whom he had hardly exchanged a sentence during his three years of employment at Service1st.

What could use improvement? The team members who were split among several teams didn't like their situation. They were unable to concentrate on one set of work, and they found it hard to determine how to allocate their time to each team so that they would be available when they were needed. Most teams were also displeased with their cubicles. Even though they had initially thought that they wanted the privacy of cubicles, they eventually began to feel that the walls were getting in the way of their collaboration. All of the teams felt that they lacked the optimum skills to accomplish their work—several teams were short on testers, and several other teams were short on writers.

Everyone then looked at Hal and his managers. How were they going to solve these problems? Whenever possible, I recommend that a team devise its own solutions to its problems; team members are closer to the work than anyone else and can come up with the best solution. We had just gone through the inspection part of an empirical process; what did they want the teams to do to adapt? The natural tendency of managers is to figure out how to do things right and tell the workers to do it that way; teams expect this. But the former managers were now ScrumMasters, and the teams were responsible for their own management. The ScrumMasters were only there to act as advisors or to help the conversation along. Once they realized this, the teams started looking for their own solutions to their problems.

The teams struggled to find overall solutions, but every solution that was proposed would help only in the short term. As work progressed, the Product Backlog would change, and different team compositions would be necessary. I told the teams that they would be hard-pressed to come up with more long-term solutions; any solution they devised would probably be good for only one or two Sprints. Circumstances would probably have changed so much by then that new solutions would be needed. This is one of the great truths of Scrum: constant inspection and adaptation are necessary for successful development.

The teams broke into smaller groups and devised the following improvements: The teams would adjust their workloads so that no one had to be assigned to multiple teams. If they found this to be impossible, the critical resource would serve only in an advisory role on the other team and would commit only to his or her primary team. To address the problem of a shortage of all cross-functional skills, they decided to try helping each other more. The tester, coder, writer, and designer would all take a first pass at the functionality design. Then the tester would flesh out the details as test scripts, while the writer started documenting and the coder started coding. The designer would tie together the results of this work so that when the code was done, the test was ready and the help system was in place for that function. To reduce the overall time required for testing and retesting the functionality, the teams decided to start using test-driven development practices with automated unit testing harnesses.

The teams weren't completely satisfied with these solutions; they didn't think that they would solve all of their problems. Nonetheless, the time allocated for the Sprint retrospective meeting had passed. I told the teams that they would never achieve perfection, no matter how much planning they did. Even though they were closer to the work than their managers had ever been, planning more than 30 days in advance is nearly impossible. However, because the teams were responsible for managing themselves, they were free to make adaptations during the Sprint. We'd inspect how things had gone at the next Sprint retrospective meeting and then make necessary adaptations again.

Lessons Learned

I keep thinking that I've learned the benefits of empirical process control with its reliance on frequent inspection and adaptation to stay on course and deliver the best possible product. But my training in defined management keeps rearing its ugly head. Deep down, I continue to believe it is my responsibility to lay things out perfectly at the beginning and then insist that the plan is adhered to. When adjustment is necessary, I feel that it's my fault for not getting everything right the first time. But Scrum rules save me from myself. It is not the Scrum-Master's job to manage the Team. The Team has to learn to manage itself, to constantly adjust its methods in order to optimize its chances of success. The Sprint retrospective provides a time for such inspection and adaptation. As with many other Scrum practices, the Sprint retrospective is time-boxed to stop the Team from spending too much time searching for perfection when no such thing exists in this complex, imperfect world.

A rule of thumb that I've adopted over my years of Scrum implementation is this: let the Team figure things out on its own. The ScrumMaster role ensures that this will happen, since the role includes no authority over the Team. The ScrumMaster is responsible for the process and removing impediments but is not responsible for managing the development of functionality. ScrumMasters can help by asking questions and providing advice, but within the guidelines, conventions, and standards of the organization, the Team is responsible for figuring out how to conduct its work. The ScrumMaster's job is to ensure that the Scrum practices are followed. Working together, the ScrumMaster and the Team shape the development process so that it will bring about the best possible results and won't let things get too far off track.

Estimating Workload: The Transition

We had finished conducting the Sprint review meeting. The ScrumMaster was wrapping up by inviting comments from the stakeholders. Peter, a Service1st founder, was particularly pleased with the progress; he finally knew what he would be getting well before the end of the release development cycle. However, he didn't like that the Team would sometimes deliver more or less than it had initially estimated it could do. This imprecision left him uneasy, and when he found out that the Team wasn't recording the actual hours each team member worked on each task in the Sprint Backlog, he was more uneasy. He wanted to know how the team would be able to compare estimated hours to actual hours worked if it wasn't recording actual hours worked. Such a comparison would give the Team valuable feedback, he felt, and might help it improve its estimates in the future. As Team estimates improved, the Team's work would be more predictable, and there would be fewer surprises.

Many people love Scrum's frequent, regular delivery of working functionality, the high morale of the team members, the improved working conditions, and the excellent quality of the systems. But phrases such as "the art of the possible" drive them crazy when they see its implications. Some hit at the heart of the misuse of the word "estimate." I saw this misuse recently in a board meeting, when a vice president of marketing shouted at the vice president of development, "How can I ever trust you when you never meet your estimates?"

To estimate means to form an approximate judgment or opinion of the value of a measure, but that wasn't the definition that was being used.

Many business relationships are based on contracts and predictability that don't tolerate the imprecision inherent in an estimate. When a salesperson says that his or her company will deliver a new release that handles a customer problem in June, a contract is formed. The customer believes that the salesperson has adequately understood his or her needs and translated them into requirements and specifications and that functionality solving his or her problem will be delivered with the release in June. The imprecision of the communication from customer to salesperson to marketing to development to a designer to a coder to a tester to a system that does what the customer wants is immense. Combine this imprecision with all of the other imprecise communication of expectations, with the imprecision and truculence of the technology being used, and with the fact that people are doing the work, and any estimate of a release date becomes suspect.

How then do we get anything done? Business and most other processes rely on some degree of predictability, and we've just posed a problem that seems to defy predictability. As you'll remember from the discussion of empirical and defined process control in Chapter 1, the problem was framed as follows:

It is typical to adopt the defined (theoretical) modeling approach when the underlying mechanisms by which a process operates are reasonably well understood. When the process is too complicated for the defined approach, the empirical approach is the appropriate choice.
> —D. A. Ogunnaike and W. H. Ray, Process Dynamics, Modeling, and Control *(Oxford University Press, 1992), p. 364*

Scrum's implementation of the empirical approach is through inspection and adaptation. All of the stakeholders are brought together every month to inspect progress on the system and to determine whether it meets their perceived needs, addressing their highest priority needs first. To the extent that the process of translating the requirements into the demonstrated increment of functionality doesn't meet their needs, the process, people, technology, or requirements are adapted to be more effective.

How Estimates Improve with Scrum

A Team's first Sprint is the roughest and most imprecise. Often this is the first time the team members have worked together, and certainly this is the first time they have worked together on this problem. The problem described in the

Product Backlog might be well known to the Team, but often it requires more understanding. The technology being employed by the Team has sometimes been used before, but often at least one new piece of technology or new release is thrown into the project. As the Team sits in this stew of imprecision and complexity, we ask the Team to commit to how much it can deliver in a 30-day Sprint. We ask the team members to tell us this within the eight-hour time-box of the Sprint planning meeting. Of course their estimate is going to be off!

We accept that the Team's estimate will be imprecise in the first Sprint. Team members delivering something approximating their commitment in the first Sprint is a testimony to human pride and determination—not the Team's estimating accuracy. I see this happen over and over. We accept the Team demonstrating more or less than that to which it committed because we know the complexities with which it is wrestling. The complexities usually stop anything from getting done. Scrum is often brought in when projects have failed, and the primary cause of failure is that the projects are floundering in the complexity. The failed projects are unable to get going. Scrum rewards action, rewarding a Team for just delivering something. Scrum asks the Team to tackle the complexity and deliver something. We limit the amount of complexity the Team is asked to tackle by time-boxing the work in a 30-day Sprint. And teams deliver. In my experience, when the imprecision and unpredictability of the effort are accepted, teams are willing to proceed and do their best. The job of the stakeholders is to accept the imprecision. The imprecision is worrisome, but it is inherent in the problem of software development.

How do we deliver releases on time that meet customer needs if the problem domain is this imprecise? Part of the answer is that estimates do get better. As the Team works together building the requirements into functionality on the selected technology, they get better. They unearth more of the unknowns. By the third or fourth Sprint, Teams are able to deliver pretty much what they commit to during the Sprint planning meeting. However, complexities still occur and disrupt this improved accuracy.

The rest of the answer is that the Product Owner and all stakeholders are responsible for figuring out what to do given how much functionality is delivered every Sprint. Given what the Team has delivered, what should the release consist of? Given how quickly or slowly the Team is turning Product Backlog into increments of functionality, when does it make sense to implement or release a set of the functionality? The Product Owner and stakeholders are driving the development cycle by trading off functionality and time. If they execute more Sprints, they can have more functionality. If they execute fewer Sprints, they will have less functionality. Or maybe they can add more Teams and determine how much this will increase the delivery of functionality. All of these decisions are adaptations that the Product Owner and stakeholders are making based on their inspection of what the Team actually does, not what it estimates it can do.

What Happens If Actuals Are Compared to Estimates

People are very complex, and often they don't do what we want them to do. I remember a situation at a large computer manufacturer that sold a very complicated high-speed printing system. Although the printing system could print reports very quickly, it kept breaking down. Customer engineers (CEs) worked many hours at customer sites keeping the printing systems working and the customers happy. But the computer manufacturer's management wasn't happy. The number of hours that the CEs were working was too costly, and the printing system division was losing money. To remedy the problem, management implemented new measurements: CEs were given bonuses based on how little time they spent repairing equipment. But to ensure that this didn't impact customer satisfaction, the CE bonuses also depended on customer satisfaction. After implementing this new bonus system, management was pleased that the cost of CEs working on problems dropped dramatically, and customer satisfaction stayed high. Several months went by before someone in management noticed that the cost of parts had skyrocketed during this time. Upon investigation, it turned out that the CEs were stocking entire subsystems at each customer site. Rather than fixing problems and repairing equipment, they would immediately replace anything that didn't work with a new subsystem.

People in software development teams are the same. When management tells them that it wants them to improve the accuracy of their estimates, what they hear is that management doesn't want any surprises. Some organizations try to improve estimates by first building databases of actual and estimated hours worked and then deriving statistics of the variances. For example, such statistics might show that a team worked 24 percent more hours than it estimated across four Sprints. Management naturally sees this as a problem. Management might then create a system of rewards if the team can reduce this imprecision. Management might tell the team that part of its performance review will depend on improving this variance to less than 20 percent. Once this target has been established, I guarantee that the team members will meet it because their salaries depend on improving this metric. Their success will cause management to view them favorably and perhaps promote them or give them more interesting work. Regardless, good things will come if the team members do what management wants. The typical way that team members then improve estimating accuracy is to drop quality or to implement the functionality with less quality. They might stop refactoring out duplicate code. They might not follow standards. They might implement a control that is less difficult but that isn't as user friendly. They might not rationalize the database. None of these actions are visible to management. All of these tricks are employed to meet the measurements and for the team members to do well in management's eyes.

Lessons Learned

The problem I've described here is called "suboptimal measurement." If you focus on improving only one part of a system, you might cause another part of the system to go haywire. The overall result is then worse than before. However, if you measure the right things, improvements can be made. In this case, increasing the accuracy of estimating by comparing actual hours worked to estimated hours worked is a suboptimal measurement. Comparing what the Team actually produces to a desired release date and release goals is a much more appropriate measurement.

For inspection and adaptation to work, we must know what we are inspecting. If we tell a Team that it can only demonstrate quality and actual working functionality, the Team will comply, and we will know real progress on delivering a release. If we tell a Team that we want it to improve the accuracy of its estimates, it will improve this metric regardless of the shortcuts it takes. Scrum asks management to focus on the overall delivery of functionality and eschew suboptimal measurements.

Peter is on track in wanting to improve estimates. To his surprise, they will improve naturally, Sprint by Sprint, as the Team becomes more competent in dealing with the technology, the business domain, and each other. What Peter needs to remember is the overall measurement—delivering the best system possible on the most appropriate date, and with excellent quality. All other measurements must be carefully implemented so that they support this overall measurement rather than undercut it. We must always factor into our measurement systems an awareness of the innate human desire to please, often regardless of the consequences.

I've mentioned many times already that Scrum is difficult. It requires frequent inspection and adaptation because these are the only known control mechanisms for complex problems. Management finally starts to understand and love Scrum when it comes to accept this and accept that this hard work is part and parcel of complex problem solving.

Learning to Have Fun While Working: The Transition

The first tour I took of the engineering space at Service1st was downright depressing. People were either housed in offices with closed doors or exiled to cubicles. Most people were alone in their offices or cubicles, often staring at a computer monitor. There was no conversation, no hum of activity, no feeling of a group of people undertaking work that they were excited to do. A lethal arrangement of space and walls had isolated the employees of Service1st.

The development process at Service1st, a standard waterfall approach with all of the attendant documentation, also isolated the company's employees. Designers designed and then wrote design documents. Programmers read the design documents and then programmed; they were allowed to ask the designers questions, if they absolutely needed to, but they were discouraged from asking too many, as this would interrupt the next set of design work. When the programmer had finished, he or she would give the specification document and code to a tester. The tester would try to find things wrong with the code, documenting any deficiencies and failures in a bug database. The programmer would inspect the bug database and fix errors; programmers could question the testers if they didn't understand the bug report, but too much interruption would disrupt the testing process, so this too was frowned upon.

The isolation was a consequence of the development process at Service1st, which minimized human interaction and face-to-face communication. The process demanded written communication between people who needed high-bandwidth communication to minimize misunderstandings and the consequent errors. People were not only physically isolated, but the development process isolated their work and interactions as well.

Everything felt different by the time the second Sprint review rolled around, and it was clear that there was positive change afoot by the subsequent Sprint retrospective. People were talking and sharing; laughter and lively conversation filled the workspace. I heard detailed questions and responses. I heard a buzz that filled the entire floor and people engaged with each other in mutually working to understand and solve problems. A common theme during the Sprint retrospective was how much the team members enjoyed working on this project. You could see it in the team members' body language. Everyone was relaxed, bantering, comfortable with being themselves around each other. The team constituted a community unto itself.

Lessons Learned

It is a now a real pleasure to visit Service1st. I walk in and people greet me, as they also greet each other. Hallways are places for conversations, not just paths for going from your car to your cubicle. Plans are already under way to rearrange and ultimately to demolish the cubicles. Employees had previously treasured their walls and the privacy they afforded. Hal changed the process and got a new neighborhood. He changed the process and got people who look forward to showing up in the morning to work with their friends and peers.

Giving the Team a Chance at WebNewSite

Scrum, combined with Extreme Programming, includes productivity-enhancing practices that increase Team productivity by orders of magnitude. One practice that slowly and then exponentially adds productivity to the Team is its commitment to its work and the team members' commitments to each other. A Team says that it will do something, and it does whatever it can to do so. Team members commit to each other that they will do something, and they help each other out whenever necessary. Early on, someone told me that he had been afraid that Scrum would promote heroics; once he experienced Scrum, however, he realized that the heroics fostered were Team heroics. Let's see what happens to a Scrum Team when a commitment fails.

Background

WebNewSite was one of the first publishers of news on the Internet through its NewsWeb product. The key to its competitive edge was its lexical parsing engine. Taking feeds from many sources, it would quickly parse the information so that it could be retrieved by category, by time, by subject, by keyword, and almost anything else that you could think of. This engine had been devised and developed by Jeff Sutherland, the other creator of Scrum, and Thomas Sun, a reclusive MIT Ph.D. Jeff had moved on to head WebNewSite's development organization, while Thomas remained the brain trust for the lexical parsing engine.

During its very first Sprint, the engineering team at WebNewSite had added a personalization facility to NewsWeb. Not only could subscribers get news, but they could also identify the types of news that they wanted to see by category and subject. Upon its release into production at the end of the first Sprint, personalization helped NewsWeb maintain its stature as a leading-edge Internet news product.

For the second Sprint, the people at WebNewSite had something up their sleeves that the competition would find hard to duplicate. The flexibility of the lexical parsing engine allowed them to also parse the news by source. Subscribers could say that they wanted to receive only international news from a given wire service, whereas local news could come from any source. During the Sprint planning meeting, the team decided that it could readily offer this capability, but Thomas Sun would have to be part of the team, a fellow pig committing himself to the team's Sprint Goals. After some discussion of what this meant to Thomas and the team, Thomas committed himself. He assured everyone that he would get right on the customization of the lexical parsing engine so that testing of extracts from the database could happen early in the Sprint.

Thomas kept his word. He had finished within a week and had tested the additional parsing. He demonstrated it to the team, and everyone felt comfortable that the Sprint goal was within the team's grasp. Thomas then dropped the bombshell. As one of the founders of WebNewSite, he hadn't had a vacation in two years. He was planning on taking some much needed time off starting the next Monday. He and his wife were going hiking in Yellowstone National Park and would be gone for two weeks. But not to worry, he said: he knew what he had accomplished, he was sure that it worked, and the results had been well-tested by the other team members.

Three days after Thomas departed, the lexical parsing engine started hiccupping, and then it had a stroke. New permutations in the news feeds had uncovered flaws in Thomas's work. Thomas was somewhere in the wilderness, completely unavailable to the team. The team's mood went from despair to fury. How could the team members meet their commitment and release what the sales department had already been promising to the public? How could Thomas have done this to them? Hadn't he understood that they were committed? Why hadn't he left a way to be reached so that he could help them and direct them to the fix?

The Sprint felt dead. As ScrumMaster, I could have called for an abnormal termination of Sprint. Circumstances had changed so that the Sprint goal appeared to be unobtainable. I just couldn't do this, though. WebNewSite had just started with Scrum; I had told them that the ScrumMaster removed impediments. This was certainly an impediment—Thomas couldn't be reached. The more I thought about it, the more I felt that this was unacceptable. Even though Thomas hadn't left a phone number, I was sure that he wouldn't want to leave the team in the lurch and that he would want to immediately come to the team's aid if he only knew of its predicament. But how could I contact him?

Unfortunately for Thomas and his vacation plans, I'm a fan of mystery novels. "Of course!" I thought. "I'll hire a private detective to find Thomas." After some searching, I found an ex-FBI agent who had an office in Billings, Montana. He was excited about working for an Internet startup. He found Thomas within two days. Thomas was able to assist the team, and the Sprint goal was met. I figured that I had been pretty inventive, spending only several hundred dollars to get around a major impediment in an unconventional manner.

Lessons Learned

I had done my work as ScrumMaster, and the team had met its commitment. Thomas, however, was steamed. Upon returning from his vacation, he stormed into the office that I was sharing with the team and read me the riot act. Who did I think I was to invade his privacy? Who was I to give his personal information to an outsider? (I had given his name and social security number to the private detective.) Who was I to expose him and his private vacation to the public like this? Circumstances were irrelevant; his privacy had been irreparably compromised.

In the end, Thomas and I agreed to disagree. I felt justified by the result, but realized that the means were pretty extreme. Thomas realized that the means, although inconsiderate, had helped his company and the team meet an important commitment. As ScrumMaster, I had weighed overall Team good against individual good and chosen. Had I chosen correctly? Everyone had a different opinion, but you'll find yourself making similar choices about the Team's welfare.

Conclusions

When Service1st started using Scrum, the organization consisted of individuals working on their assigned tasks in isolated workspaces. A friend of mine, thinking about the idea of collocated Team work areas, remarked that when he was a child and had been bad, his parents put him in a corner. He had to face away from everyone and be in isolation. He couldn't help but notice the parallel between this punishment for being bad and what we do to our most valuable assets, our employees.

When people are asked to achieve the possible, they will often try. When people are asked to try to do a little more than the possible, they will continue to try if they aren't punished for not achieving everything. When people are given all the help they need and ask for, when people are encouraged and treasured, they almost always respond by doing their best.

When people work by themselves, they can achieve great things. When people work with others, they often achieve synergy, where the joint effort far exceeds the sum of the individual efforts. In my experience, this exponential increase in productivity continues until a Team reaches seven people, give or take two. At that point, the shared work, vision, and concepts start to require additional support, such as documentation. Regardless of the scaling mechanism, above a modest number like seven, the productivity of a Team starts to decline, the miscommunications increase, the mistakes proliferate, and frustration grows.

Scrum is for achieving results in complex situations. Using practices such as the Product Backlog, the results can be optimized to the situation. But Scrum is also very much about people. ScrumMasters become dedicated to their teams because teams are neighborhoods that people, including the ScrumMaster, live within.

When I last visited Service1st, it was a good place to visit. I could watch people striving to improve the organization, the teams, themselves, and their profession. I was proud to be associated with them. I have helped implement Scrum in hundreds of organizations over the last decade, and I found this to be a reasonable outcome to anticipate. What more can you ask from life?

9

Scaling Projects Using Scrum

Many projects require more effort than a single Scrum Team can provide. In these circumstances, multiple Teams can be employed. Working in parallel, the efforts of these Teams are coordinated through a variety of mechanisms that range from formal to ad hoc. When more than one Scrum Team works simultaneously on a project, it is referred to as a *scaled project*, and the mechanisms employed to coordinate the work of these teams are called *scaling mechanisms*. Every scaled project has its own complexities, each of which usually requires its own unique solution. Scrum scales in the same manner as any other development process, using practically the same scaling mechanisms, while retaining all of the empirical practices that form its core. This chapter provides guidelines for scaling projects using Scrum; these patterns are ones that I've used successfully on nearly a hundred projects. But keep in mind that scaling can be difficult, and remember that this chapter doesn't offer any magic formulas or foolproof prescriptions.

The kernel around which all scaling occurs is the Scrum Team. An 800-person project will consist of one hundred 8-person teams. In this chapter, we'll examine how to coordinate the work of these teams while maintaining the productivity of each individual Scrum Team. We'll also examine how to scale projects regardless of the number of people they involve, as well as the type of application, the type of system, the number of places in which development is to occur, and other relevant scaling dimensions. In this chapter, I will demonstrate the employment of Scrum scaling practices in a mission-critical project where the pressure to scale to a large project was intense. In this case, the scaling had to support multiple teams working simultaneously on one software system from multiple geographic locations.

Scaling at MegaFund

We've looked at MegaFund in previous chapters. MegaFund had a pressing business problem that it wanted to solve as quickly as possible. If you were a MegaFund customer in 1997 and wanted to transfer money, open an account, trade stock, or take advantage of any of MegaFund's other financial offerings, you had two choices: you could either pick up the telephone and call an agent or go to the MegaFund office in the nearest metropolitan area and use a dumb 3270-type terminal connected through a network to MegaFund's mainframes. Although this technology had been innovative in the 1980s, MegaFund competitors now let customers manage their accounts themselves from their home or office computers, cell phones, Web-based devices, pagers, and telephone voice-response units, at any time and on any day. The pressure to correct this competitive disparity and provide competitive technology was immense at MegaFund. Everyone at MegaFund wanted to start his or her own project and immediately build a competitive offering.

Approach

MegaFund Systems Company (MSC) provided technology services to Mega-Fund. MSC determined that the best way to support the new competitive products was to link them to its legacy databases through middleware servers. Every organization would write its own business functionality to run on the servers, and MSC would write common data access capabilities. The servers would be designed to support virtually any transaction volumes in a secure, restartable environment. These goals constituted the first nonfunctional requirements that were put in the Product Backlog.

The Product Owner wanted to initiate many teams so that solutions could be delivered as soon as possible. However, if architecture with adequate details wasn't present first, the work couldn't be cleanly divided among the multiple teams. If a development environment supporting multi-site source code management and build processes wasn't set before work began, the multiple Teams would get out of sync and would likely create conflicting code. And if standards weren't defined before work began, the interfaces between the business and data objects would likely be inconsistent. Consequently, we defined a nonfunctional Product Backlog to devise and construct such a scalability infrastructure. All of these nonfunctional requirements were given top priority.

We then added a small number of functional business requirements. The account management organization wanted customers to be able to directly access their accounts and review balances and previous transactions over the Web. We broke these requirements down into smaller pieces and parsed them among the nonfunctional requirements, planning to build part of the account management functionality every Sprint while putting the scaling infrastructure and materials in place. To staff this team, we selected some of the best designers and architects at MegaFund. Because the Product Backlog required standards and infrastructure development, we also staffed the team with writers and infrastructure and build engineers. As a result, the team was somewhat oversized at 10 people.

At the end of the first Sprint, the team demonstrated a single account management transaction: the team showed existing balances, working from a Web browser, through transaction-specific business objects, to information-specific data objects, through the legacy databases, and back. The team then demonstrated the transaction after restarting the server, as would happen in the event of a crash. Several team members showed scalability figures extrapolating the performance of this single transaction across multiple transactions on clusters of the selected server technology. In sum, the team demonstrated that its approach was viable by using it to successfully execute a business transaction.

The Product Owner and other stakeholders were so delighted that they wanted to immediately create more teams and set them loose on this project. However, the initial team required two more Sprints to complete the scaling infrastructure, so it wasn't until the fourth Sprint that more teams were created. There were now seven teams sprinting, each of which was seeded with someone from the initial team who was charged with providing expertise and guidance to the rest of the team. Each team conducted Daily Scrums, which were followed by a "Daily Scrum of Scrums" at which the members of the initial team met as representatives of their new teams to synchronize the work of these seven new teams. The Daily Scrum of Scrums followed the same format as a regular Daily Scrum.

Lessons Learned

This MegaFund project delivered valuable business functionality from the very first Sprint. Even though three Sprints were required before we could scale the project to seven teams, the stakeholders in the project saw progress being made on their problem from the start. They had to hold themselves back from scaling too quickly, but they were never left feeling that important progress wasn't being made. The Teams delivered business value to the Product Owners at every Sprint review, and the Product Owners were beside themselves with delight. Sometimes it is difficult for teams to break down complex technical or business problems into something that can be demonstrated within a Sprint, but I've yet to see a team fail this challenge.

It is worth underscoring several Scrum practices used in this example that are critical to the success of any scaling effort. First, build the infrastructure for scaling prior to scaling. Second, always deliver business value while building the infrastructure. Third, optimize the capabilities of the initial team, and then staff the additional teams with at least one member of the initial team. These practices are described in more detail in the next section.

Scrum Scaling

Prior to scaling any project, an appropriate infrastructure must be put in place. For instance, if a project will employ multiple collocated teams, a mechanism for frequently synchronizing their work must be devised and implemented. Also, a more detailed product and technical architecture must be constructed so that the work can be cleanly divided among the teams. If these teams are to be geographically distributed, high-bandwidth technology for source code sharing, synchronized builds, and alternative communications such as instant messaging must be employed.

Everything that supports the scaling effort must be devised and implemented prior to the scaling of the project; all of this work is done in Sprints. But Scrum requires that every Sprint produce an increment of potentially shippable product functionality, and you might be asking how this requirement can be met if months are needed to devise and implement a scaling infrastructure. Indeed, even though less business functionality will be created during these initial Sprints to build infrastructure, it is still necessary to demonstrate some business functionality at the end of these Sprints. In fact, it is all the more important to do so because this allows the infrastructure to be tested with functionality development work as it evolves. Demonstrating business functionality also enables the production of the kind of results that the Product Owner and stakeholders value so highly from the very start and goes a long way toward keeping them engaged in the project.

The nonfunctional requirements to build the scaling infrastructure are given high priority in the Product Backlog because theymust be completed before scaling begins in earnest. Because business functionality must be demonstrated at the end of every Sprint, these nonfunctional requirements are mixed with top-priority business functionality, and sometimes even outrank that functionality. If a piece of business functionality is dependent on a nonfunctional requirement, the nonfunctional requirement must be prioritized in the Product Backlog so that it is developed prior to or in parallel with the business functionality. The more scaling is required, the more the top-priority Product Backlog will be heavily skewed toward nonfunctional requirements for scaling. In such instances, more effort will be expended on preparation and less on direct business value until the scaling infrastructure is in place.

The process of defining and prioritizing the nonfunctional requirements for scaling is called *staging*. Staging occurs prior to the start of the first Sprint and takes just one day. During this day, the nonfunctional scaling requirements for this particular project are determined and placed in the Product Backlog. For example, if you are scaling the project to use multiple teams, the following nonfunctional requirements should be added to the Product Backlog:

- Decompose business architecture to support clean-interface multi-team development.

- Decompose system architecture to support clean-interface multi-team development.

- If necessary, define and implement a development environment to support multi-team collocated or distributed environments.

After these nonfunctional requirements for scaling are placed in the Product Backlog, Sprints can begin. However, only one team can sprint until the scaling infrastructure is in place, as there of course will be no mechanism for coordinating the work of multiple teams in the meantime. See Figure 9-1 for a representation of the initial Product Backlog with all nonfunctional requirements appropriate for the type of staging envisioned. The Product Owner and Team get together at a Sprint planning meeting and collaborate to select a combination of functional and nonfunctional requirements. The Team then sprints as many times as required until the infrastructure for the staging is in place. At this point, the Sprint planning meetings for each of the multiple Sprint Teams can be held. Each new Team is seeded with a member of the original Team, who serves as the new Team's expert on the project's infrastructure and architecture.

These practices are some of those that were required to scale a Y2K project that was undertaken in the late 1990s. During this period, almost every organization was trying to ensure that its software was Y2K-compliant and wouldn't cause problems upon the dawn of the twenty-first century. In the next section, I will describe how an organization used Scrum scaling techniques to orchestrate a large project aimed at upgrading its software for Y2K and then helping customers implement the new release.

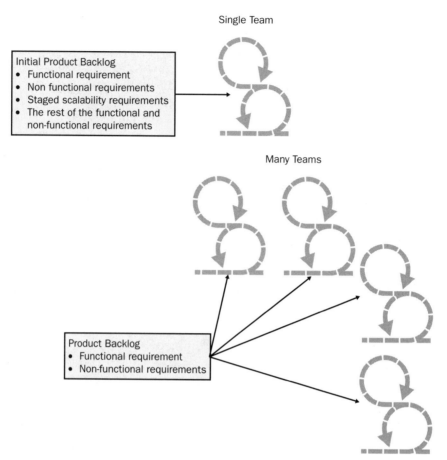

Figure 9-1 Scalability Sprints

Scaling at Medcinsoft

Scrum was used at Medcinsoft to manage a Y2K project aimed at making Medcinsoft's products Y2K-compliant, providing releases of this software to over 350 major healthcare organizations and teaching hospitals (customers), and stabilizing these releases before October 1, 1999. Medcinsoft's software ran the administrative aspects of healthcare organizations, including admissions, discharges, billing, insurance, patient records, and receivables. The failure of such software would have had catastrophic consequences for these organizations and the populations they serve. Until Medcinsoft adopted Scrum, it had been using Gantt charts to manage the project, and they had proven woefully inadequate to the task. Customers were dissatisfied because releases regularly arrived months late, were horrifically buggy, and didn't contain desired features.

The project was complex and required scaling in a number of dimensions simultaneously. The software development, Y2K remediation, and bug fixing of over 300 developers of various product lines had to be prioritized and coordinated. Over 400 field support staff needed to have their work and communications with Medcinsoft customers prioritized and coordinated. Over 600 employees at the 350 customer organizations needed to be able to communicate plans and changes in these plans to Medcinsoft. Customers were operating various releases of Medcinsoft software, most of which were customized to their specific needs. All of the customers had different timetables for the implementation of the Y2K upgrade of Medcinsoft software, each of which took into account their plans to upgrade other software they used on site. Customers also had specific schedules for executing extensive testing of their new systems. In sum, customer timetables, knowledge bases, and skill levels varied widely.

Scrum had been used successfully elsewhere within Medcinsoft, so management asked Jack Hart, the manager of the Y2K project, whether he could use Scrum to help the Y2K project along. The most pressing problems that Jack had to address were the complexity of coordinating all of the work being done and the variability of timing in the different parts of that work. To coordinate the work being done, he needed accurate, timely information. Planning information from the customers came in sporadically and was oftentimes contradictory. Release status information was unreliable, and releases often weren't ready until weeks after they were supposed to be shipped. Customers and field service personnel weren't communicating with each other at all or weren't communicating effectively with each other.

Each customer's schedule for testing Medcinsoft's software was tied to the testing of other software and software packages, and those plans were in turn tied to training and rollout plans, all of which had to be completed before the start of Y2K. Medcinsoft had to deliver its new release on time, but it also had to be able to change its delivery date if customers experienced any changes in their schedule. Each Medcinsoft release had to include software that was completely tested, with all of the known Y2K remediation work completed, with critical and high-priority bugs resolved, and with any outstanding defects documented. This release had to be implemented at the customer site, and any previously customized code would be identified and implemented in the release by Medcinsoft field personnel. Finally, the Medcinsoft release had to be integrated with and interfaced to other software in use at the customer site.

As though this weren't enough, Jack had further complications. Despite having previously conducted extensive searches for Y2K defects in accordance with industry and internal guidelines, new Y2K defects were still being found on a regular basis. Also, Medcinsoft planned to integrate new Web access functionality into the Y2K release. Operational defects resulting from the Web enhancement proved difficult to detect, and as defects were corrected, other bugs were often created. Parts of the software were practically ancient; because yesterday's developers—the ones who had written the code—were no longer around to help rewrite it, today's developers had to learn the code as they upgraded it. Furthermore, the base software was over 2500 function-points in size, large by almost any standard. There were additional customer complexities in the mix, too. Many Medcinsoft customers had never performed such an extensive upgrade of their software and systems and were largely unprepared to do so. A surprising number didn't have testing and quality assurance environments or processes with which to systematically test a new release.

Approach

Scrum provides a degree of regularity or predictability in a complex or chaotic environment like that of the Medcinsoft Y2K project. Jack decided to apply Scrum to all aspects of the project, even activities in the field and at customer sites. Jack synchronized releases with each Sprint. Every 30 days, Medcinsoft would provide specific customers with a new release of software. Each Sprint would create a release that addressed top-priority Product Backlog and any critical bugs found during the Sprint. However, Jack found it difficult to acquire accurate information regarding customer priorities, implementation dates, and critical fixes in a timely manner. Field support personnel provided information about each customer's needs, and different people at the customer organization communicated with them. Jack needed a normalizing filter for this information, a way to make it timely, predictable, and accurate. To this end, he instituted Daily Scrums for customers who were within three months of requiring a Y2K release from Medcinsoft, and he instituted weekly versions of the Daily Scrum for customers whose release date was outside the three-month window. At each Daily Scrum meeting, the customer and the Medcinsoft field support personnel discussed status and issues. They maintained an updated, prioritized list of the required date for the Medcinsoft software release, customization required for that customer, customer-specific enhancements or functionality that had to be included in the release, and outstanding critical and high-priority bugs and defects at that customer site. (See Figure 9-2.) Each customer had its own list, or Product Backlog, that evolved across time.

Single Customer Product Backlog

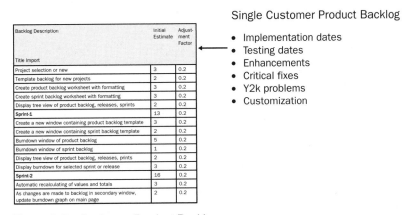

Backlog Description	Initial Estimate	Adjust- ment Factor
Title Import		
Project selection or new	3	0.2
Template backlog for new projects	2	0.2
Create product backlog worksheet with formatting	3	0.2
Create sprint backlog worksheet with formatting	3	0.2
Display tree view of product backlog, releases, sprints	2	0.2
Sprint-1	13	0.2
Create a new window containing product backlog template	3	0.2
Create a new window containing sprint backlog template	2	0.2
Burndown window of product backlog	5	0.2
Burndown window of sprint backlog	1	0.2
Display tree view of product backlog, releases, prints	2	0.2
Display burndown for selected sprint or release	3	0.2
Sprint-2	16	0.2
Automatic recalculating of values and totals	3	0.2
As changes are made to backlog in secondary window, update burndown graph on main page	2	0.2

- Implementation dates
- Testing dates
- Enhancements
- Critical fixes
- Y2k problems
- Customization

Figure 9-2   Customer Product Backlog

Whenever the customer Product Backlog changed, it was rolled into Medcinsoft district and divisional Product Backlogs in the Medcinsoft field service organization. This combined Product Backlog was then prioritized to reflect scheduling among all of the customers. This combined Product Backlog was known as the "field service Product Backlog." Field service management used it to plan and allocate field service personnel to perform customizations and assist in the implementation, testing, and rollout of the software.

The Medcinsoft development Product Backlog consisted of Y2K fixes, product enhancements, bugs found in testing, and other high-priority development environment work. When the field service Product Backlog was merged with the development Product Backlog, the result was an overall Medcinsoft Y2K Product Backlog, which was used to prioritize and direct the overall Y2K efforts. Development work was prioritized based on Y2K objectives and specific customer requirements, with all priorities driven by dates. This Product Backlog supported the various customer implementations and directed all Medcinsoft and customer work. (See Figure 9-3.) The Medcinsoft Y2K Product Backlog was updated every day.

The customer, district, division, development, and overall Y2K Product Backlogs were maintained on spreadsheets on a public server and could be accessed through the Web by everyone involved in the project. This required quite a lot of cooperation and communication, as the spreadsheet could only be updated by one workstation at a time. However, the people at Medcinsoft felt that this solution worked well enough, and they appreciated that it made their Y2K commitments and priorities visible. Everyone appreciated being able to plainly see how work was allocated and how release content was scheduled.

Regional   District

Customer

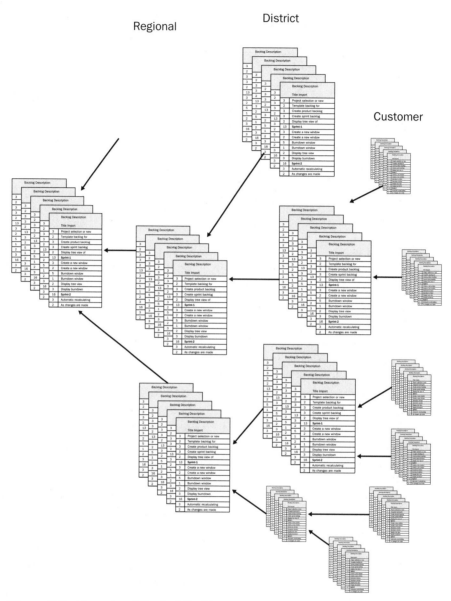

Figure 9-3 Hierarchy of Product Backlogs

    The field service organization was responsible for coordinating and conducting all work at customer sites. Judy was a district manager who had been brought to headquarters to help with the Y2K project. She assumed the Scrum Product Owner role and maintained the overall Y2K Product Backlog of work and kept it prioritized. She maintained the list by asking the following question: "When do customers need a release with Y2K defects fixed and any other requested functionality?" For instance, the subset of top-priority Product Backlog at the start of a Sprint might look like this:

- Defect of report header printing date incorrectly in module or report.

- Defect of screen in module patient demographic displaying year incorrectly.

- Module patient demographic freezes when year 2010 entered in date field.

- New plug-in module from software vendor to fix rollover date problem.

- Bug—screen address change of module patient demographic doesn't return to correct prior page.

- Customer MediLife requires release for implementation (currently running release 8.1).

- Customer MedClinic requires release for implementation (currently running release 7.2).

Development teams were grouped by functionality, such as BAR (Billing, Accounts Receivable), SCHED (Scheduling), and so on. (See Figure 9-4.) At Sprint planning meetings, the team in question worked with Judy to select for its next Sprint the Product Backlog that was within its functional domain. The team members had worked at Medcinsoft long enough so that who was responsible was rarely in dispute. If not enough work was available to fully load the team, the team would allocate only an estimated percentage of its time to the Y2K project during that Sprint and would work on other projects during its remaining time. Jack used this approach to keep work parsed cleanly, since up to 20 teams of up to 10 members could be simultaneously working on the Product Backlog. These teams included functional teams, build teams, Y2K-defect detection teams, quality assurance (QA) teams, and release teams.

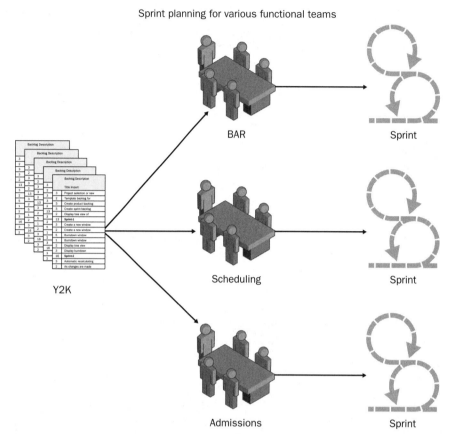

Figure 9-4   Sprint planning for multiple teams

The same scaling mechanisms were used for the Web access project, which consisted of completely new functionality and code that was to be included in the Y2K release. This project began with rather extensive system architecture and design Sprints. The result of each Sprint was some working functionality as well as an increasingly detailed system design that was used to keep the various Web access teams from tripping over each other.

Bug Fixing

During each Sprint, bugs were entered into a defect tracking system. Some of these bugs were caught as a testing team regression-tested the "being built" increment. Some of the bugs were Y2K bugs that were detected during further Y2K remediation testing. Some of the bugs cropped up as customers tested and implemented their own Y2K releases. Medcinsoft's initial intent was to fix all bugs and defects prior to the final Y2K release. This proved unrealistic, however, as many customers wanted to "batten down the hatches" well before the start of the year 2000. To accommodate these earlier implementation dates and improve the integrity of each release, Judy reviewed new bugs prior to Daily Scrums and added all critical and high-priority bugs to the Sprint Backlog for the various teams working on that release. This was a violation of the Scrum rule that no outside work will be added to a team's Sprint once it is under way. However, the Scrum practice of following common sense won out, because unless these defects were addressed immediately, pushing the new releases out to the field would just be asking for trouble and wasting customers' time.

Jack gave the Scrum teams the following rules for managing their own time and work. He told them that Y2K work was their highest priority. If they had allocated only 50 percent of their time to this Sprint and were working on other things the remaining 50 percent of their time, they were to drain the other 50 percent and reallocate it to working on Y2K bugs and defects until they were all resolved. Or, if the team was 100 percent–allocated to the Y2K Sprint, team members were to reach outside the team and include other engineers to help address the Y2K bugs and defects until they were all resolved.

Lessons Learned

Medcinsoft successfully navigated the shoals of this project's complexities and met its customers' needs through constant inspection, analysis, devising of solutions, and adaptation. Many of the teams involved in this project didn't develop software; they tested software, implemented software, or managed organizational activities. Yet they all used the inspection and adaptation mechanisms of Scrum to stay on top of every change.

You can get through almost anything if you don't try to impose rigid solutions before problems even arise, instead devising solutions as necessary when problems crop up. Such solutions as the hierarchical Daily Scrum of Scrums worked, and the regularity and brevity of these solutions made them easy to bear. However, it wasn't the solutions Jack devised as much as it was the simple rules that the teams followed that caused the increased, synchronized communications that ultimately saved the project. Insisting on creating a shippable release every 30 days, regardless of what happens, and making certain to frequently synchronize customer realities with Product Backlogs always kept Medcinsoft on the straight and true.

Conclusions

When I presented these case studies at a meeting of ScrumMasters in Milan in June 2003, Mel Pullen pointed out that he felt that the Scrum of Scrums practice was contrary to the Scrum practice of self-organization and self-management. Hierarchical structures are management impositions, Mel asserted, and are not optimally derived by those who are actually doing the work. Why not let each Team figure out which other Teams it has to cooperate and coordinate with and where the couplings are? Either the ScrumMaster can point out the dependency to the Team, or the Team can come across the dependency in the course of development. When a Team stumbles over the dependency, it can send people to serve as "chickens" on the Daily Scrum of the other Team working on the dependency. If no such other Team exists, the Team with the unaddressed dependency can request that a high-priority Product Backlog item be created to address it. The ScrumMaster can then either let the initial Team tackle the dependency or form another Team to do so.

This was an interesting observation. Scrum relies on self-organization as well as simple, guiding rules. Which is more applicable to coordinate and scale projects? I've tried both and found that the proper solution depends on the complexity involved. When the complexity is so great that self-organization doesn't occur quickly enough, simple rules help the organization reach a timely resolution. If self-organization occurs in a timely manner, I prefer to rely on it because management is unlikely to devise adaptations as frequently or well as the Team can. Sometimes the ScrumMaster can aid self-organization by devising a few simple rules, but it is easier for the ScrumMaster to overdo it than not do enough.

Appendix A

Rules

The ScrumMaster is responsible for ensuring that everyone related to a project, whether chickens or pigs, follows the rules of Scrum. These rules hold the Scrum process together so that everyone knows how to play. If the rules aren't enforced, people waste time figuring out what to do. If the rules are disputed, time is lost while everyone waits for a resolution. These rules have worked in literally thousands of successful projects. If someone wants to change the rules, use the Sprint retrospective meeting as a forum for discussion. Rule changes should originate from the Team, not management. Rule changes should be entertained if and only if the ScrumMaster is convinced that the Team and everyone involved understands how Scrum works in enough depth that they will be skillful and mindful in changing the rules. No rules can be changed until the ScrumMaster has determined that this state has been reached.

Sprint Planning Meeting

The Sprint planning meeting is time-boxed to 8 hours and consists of two segments that are time-boxed to 4 hours each. The first segment is for selecting Product Backlog; the second segment is for preparing a Sprint Backlog.

■ The attendees are the ScrumMaster, the Product Owner, and the Team. Additional parties can be invited by any of these people to provide additional business domain or technology domain information and advice, but they are dismissed after this information is provided. There are no chickens as observers.

■ The Product Owner must prepare the Product Backlog prior to the meeting. In the absence of either the Product Owner or the Product Backlog, the ScrumMaster is required to construct an adequate Product Backlog prior to the meeting and to stand in for the Product Owner.

■ The goal of the first segment, or first 4 hours, is for the Team to select those Product Backlog items that it believes it can commit to turning into an increment of potentially shippable product functionality. The Team will demonstrate this functionality to the Product Owner and stakeholders at the Sprint review meeting at the end of the Sprint.

■ The Team can make suggestions, but the decision of what Product Backlog can constitute the Sprint is the responsibility of the Product Owner.

■ The Team is responsible for determining how much of the Product Backlog that the Product Owner wants worked on the Team will attempt to do during the Sprint.

■ Time-boxing the first segment to 4 hours means that this is all of the time that is available for analyzing the Product Backlog. Further analysis must be performed during the Sprint. Large-grained, high-priority Product Backlog with imprecise estimates might not be thoroughly understood during this part of the Sprint planning meeting and might result in the Team not being able to complete all of the Product Backlog that it selects.

■ The second segment of the Sprint Planning meeting occurs immediately after the first segment and is also time-boxed to 4 hours.

■ The Product Owner must be available to the Team during the second segment to answer questions that the Team might have about the Product Backlog.

■ It is up to the Team, acting solely on its own and without any direction from outside the Team, to figure out during the second segment how it will turn the selected Product Backlog into an increment of potentially shippable product functionality. No one else is allowed to do anything but observe or answer questions seeking further information.

■ The output of the second segment of the Sprint planning meeting is a list, called the Sprint Backlog, of tasks, task estimates, and assignments that will start the Team on the work of developing the functionality. The task list might not be complete, but it must be complete enough to reflect mutual commitment on the part of all Team members and to carry them through the first part of the Sprint, while the Team devises more tasks in the Sprint Backlog.

Daily Scrum Meeting

The Daily Scrum meeting is time-boxed to 15 minutes regardless of the number of Team members.

- Hold the Daily Scrum in the same place at the same time every work day. The Daily Scrum is best held first thing in the day so that the first thing Team members do on arriving at work is think of what they did the day before and what they plan to do today.

- All Team members are required to attend. If for some reason a Team member can't attend in person, the absent member must either attend by telephone or by having another Team member report on the absent member's status.

- Team members must be prompt. The ScrumMaster starts the meeting at the appointed time, regardless of who is present. Any members who are late pay $1 to the ScrumMaster immediately.

- The ScrumMaster begins the meeting by starting with the person immediately to his or her left and proceeding counterclockwise around the room until everyone has reported.

- Each Team member should respond to three questions only:

  - What have you done since the last Daily Scrum regarding this project?

  - What will you do between now and the next Daily Scrum meeting regarding this project?

  - What impedes you from performing your work as effectively as possible?

- Team members should not digress beyond answering these three questions into issues, designs, discussion of problems, or gossip. The ScrumMaster is responsible for moving the reporting along briskly, from person to person.

- During the Daily Scrum, only one person talks at a time. That person is the one who is reporting his or her status. Everyone else listens. There are no side conversations.

- When a Team member reports something that is of interest to other Team members or needs the assistance of other Team members, any Team member can immediately arrange for all interested parties to get together after the Daily Scrum to set up a meeting.

- Chickens are not allowed to talk, make observations, make faces, or otherwise make their presence in the Daily Scrum meeting obtrusive.

- Chickens stand on the periphery of the Team so as not to interfere with the meeting.

- If too many chickens attend the meeting, the ScrumMaster can limit attendance so that the meeting can remain orderly and focused.

- Chickens are not allowed to talk with Team members after the meeting for clarification or to provide advice or instructions.

- Pigs or chickens who cannot or will not conform to the above rules can be excluded from the meeting (chickens) or removed from the Team (pigs).

Sprint

The Sprint is time-boxed to 30 consecutive calendar days. Aside from other factors, this is the amount of time required for a Team to build something of significant interest to the Product Owner and stakeholders and bring it to a state where it is potentially shippable. This is also the maximum time that can be allocated without the Team doing so much work that it requires artifacts and documentation to support its thought processes. It is also the maximum time that most stakeholders will wait without losing interest in the Team's progress and without losing their belief that the Team is doing something meaningful for them.

- The Team can seek outside advice, help, information, and support during the Sprint.

- No one can provide advice, instructions, commentary, or direction to the Team during the Sprint. The Team is utterly self-managing.

- The Team commits to Product Backlog during the Sprint planning meeting. No one is allowed to change this Product Backlog during the Sprint. The Product Backlog is frozen until the end of the Sprint.

- If the Sprint proves to be not viable, the ScrumMaster can abnormally terminate the Sprint and initiate a new Sprint planning meeting to initiate the next Sprint. The ScrumMaster can make this change of his or her own accord or as requested by the Team or the Product Owner. The Sprint can prove to be not viable if the technology proves unworkable, if the business conditions change so that the Sprint will not be of value to the business, or if the Team is interfered with during the Sprint by anyone outside the Team.

- If the Team feels itself unable to complete all of the committed Product Backlog during the Sprint, it can consult with the Product Owner on which items to remove from the current Sprint. If so many items require removal that the Sprint has lost its value and meaning, the ScrumMaster can abnormally terminate the Sprint, as previously stated.

- If the Team determines that it can address more Product Backlog during the Sprint than it selected during the Sprint planning meeting, it can consult with the Product Owner on which additional Product Backlog items can be added to the Sprint.

- The Team members have two administrative responsibilities during the Sprint: they are to attend the Daily Scrum meeting, and they are to keep the Sprint Backlog up-to-date and available in a public folder on a public server, visible to all. New tasks must be added to the Sprint Backlog as they are conceived, and the running, day-to-day estimated hours remaining for each task must be kept up-to-date.

Sprint Review Meeting

The Sprint review meeting is time-boxed to 4 hours.

- The Team should not spend more than 1 hour preparing for the Sprint review.

- The purpose of the Sprint review is for the Team to present to the Product Owner and stakeholders functionality that is done. Although the meaning of "done" can vary from organization to organization, it usually means that the functionality is completely engineered and could be potentially shipped or implemented. If "done" has another meaning, make sure that the Product Owner and stakeholders understand it.

- Functionality that isn't "done" cannot be presented.

- Artifacts that aren't functionality cannot be presented except when used in support of understanding the demonstrated functionality. Artifacts cannot be shown as work products, and their use must be minimized to avoid confusing stakeholders or requiring them to understand how systems development works.

- Functionality should be presented on the Team member workstations and executed from the server closest to production—usually a quality assurance (QA) environment server.

- The Sprint review starts with a Team member presenting the Sprint goal, the Product Backlog committed to, and the Product Backlog completed. Different Team members can then discuss what went well and what didn't go well in the Sprint.

- The majority of the Sprint review is spent with Team members presenting functionality, answering stakeholder questions regarding the presentation, and noting changes that are desired.

- At the end of the presentations, the stakeholders are polled, one by one, to get their impressions, any desired changes, and the priority of these changes.

- The Product Owner discusses with the stakeholders and the Team potential rearrangement of the Product Backlog based on the feedback.

- Stakeholders are free to voice any comments, observations, or criticisms regarding the increment of potentially shippable product functionality between presentations.

- Stakeholders can identify functionality that wasn't delivered or wasn't delivered as expected and request that such functionality be placed in the Product Backlog for prioritization.

- Stakeholders can identify any new functionality that occurs to them as they view the presentation and request that the functionality be added to the Product Backlog for prioritization.

- The ScrumMaster should attempt to determine the number of people who expect to attend the Sprint review meeting and set up the meeting to accommodate them.

- At the end of the Sprint review, the ScrumMaster announces the place and date of the next Sprint review to the Product Owner and all stakeholders.

Sprint Retrospective Meeting

The Sprint retrospective meeting is time-boxed to 3 hours.

- It is attended only by the Team, the ScrumMaster, and the Product Owner. The Product Owner is optional.

- Start the meeting by having all Team members answer two questions:

  ❏ What went well during the last Sprint?

  ❏ What could be improved in the next Sprint?

- The ScrumMaster writes down the Team's answers in summary form.

- The Team prioritizes in which order it wants to talk about the potential improvements.

- The ScrumMaster is not at this meeting to provide answers, but to facilitate the Team's search for better ways for the Scrum process to work for it.

- Actionable items that can be added to the next Sprint should be devised as high-priority nonfunctional Product Backlog. Retrospectives that don't result in change are sterile and frustrating.

Appendix B

Definitions

Item	Definition
Burndown graph	The trend of work remaining across time in a Sprint, a release, or a product. The source of the raw data is the Sprint Backlog and the Product Backlog, with work remaining tracked on the vertical axis and the time periods (days of a Sprint or Sprints) tracked on the horizontal axis.
Chicken	Someone who is interested in the project but does not have formal Scrum responsibilities and accountabilities (is not a Team member, Product Owner, ScrumMaster, or other stakeholder).
Daily Scrum meeting	A short status meeting held daily by each Team during which the Team members synchronize their work and progress and report any impediments to the ScrumMaster for removal.
Done	Complete as mutually agreed to by all parties and conforming to an organization's standards, conventions, and guidelines. When something is reported as "done" at the Daily Scrum or demonstrated as "done" at the Sprint review meeting, it must conform to this agreed definition.
Estimated work remaining	The number of hours that a Team member estimates remain to be worked on any task. This estimate is updated at the end of every day the Sprint Backlog task is worked on. The estimate is the total estimated hours remaining, regardless of the number of people that perform the work.
Increment	Product functionality that is developed by the Team during each Sprint.
Increment of potentially shippable product functionality	A completely developed increment that contains all of the parts of a completed product, except for the Product Backlog items that the Team selected for this Sprint.
Iteration	One cycle within a project. In Scrum, this cycle is 30 sequential calendar days, or a Sprint.
Pig	Someone occupying one of the three Scrum roles (Team, Product Owner, ScrumMaster) who has made a commitment and has the authority to fulfill it.

Item	Definition
Product Backlog	A prioritized list of project requirements with estimated times to turn them into completed product functionality. Estimates are in days and are more precise the higher an item is in the Product Backlog priority. The list evolves, changing as business conditions or technology changes.
Product Backlog items	Functional requirements, nonfunctional requirements, and issues, which are prioritized in order of importance to the business and dependencies and then estimated. The precision of the estimate depends on the priority and granularity of the Product Backlog item, with the highest priority items that can be selected in the next Sprint being very granular and precise.
Product Owner	The person responsible for managing the Product Backlog so as to maximize the value of the project. The Product Owner represents all stakeholders in the project.
Scrum	Not an acronym, but mechanisms in the game of rugby for getting an out-of-play ball back into play.
ScrumMaster	The person responsible for the Scrum process, its correct implementation, and the maximization of its benefits.
Sprint	A time-box of 30 sequential calendar days during which a Team works to turn the Product Backlog it has selected into an increment of potentially shippable product functionality.
Sprint Backlog	A list of tasks that defines a Team's work for a Sprint. The list emerges during the Sprint. Each task identifies those responsible for doing the work and the estimated amount of work remaining on the task on any given day during the Sprint.
Sprint Backlog task	One of the tasks that the Team or a Team member defines as required to turn committed Product Backlog items into system functionality.
Sprint planning meeting	A one-day meeting time-boxed to 8 hours that initiates every Sprint. The meeting is divided into two 4-hour segments, each also time-boxed. During the first segment, the Product Owner presents the highest priority Product Backlog to the Team. The Team and the Product Owner collaborate to help the Team determine how much Product Backlog it can turn into functionality during the upcoming Sprint. The Team commits to this Product Backlog at the end of the first segment. During the second segment of the meeting, the Team plans how it will meet this commitment by detailing its work as a plan in the Sprint Backlog.
Sprint retrospective meeting	A meeting time-boxed to 3 hours and facilitated by the ScrumMaster at which the Team discusses the just-concluded Sprint and determines what could be changed that might make the next Sprint more enjoyable or productive.

Item	Definition
Sprint review meeting	A meeting time-boxed to 4 hours at the end of every Sprint at which the Team demonstrates to the Product Owner and any other interested parties what it was able to accomplish during the Sprint. Only completed product functionality can be demonstrated.
Stakeholder	Someone with an interest in the outcome of a project, either because he or she has funded it, will use it, or will be affected by it.
Team	A cross-functional group of people that is responsible for managing itself to develop software every Sprint.
Time-box	A period of time that cannot be exceeded and within which an event or meeting occurs. For example, a Daily Scrum meeting is time-boxed to 15 minutes and terminates at the end of those 15 minutes, regardless.

Appendix C

Resources

The following table lists some resources that might be valuable to understanding Scrum better. Some are static resources, such as articles and books that directly address Scrum. Others contain material that helps the reader understand Scrum and Agile processes better. Other resources are dynamic sources of information regarding Scrum and Agile processes, such as Web sites and discussion groups. All of this information has been a prime mover in my understanding of Scrum.

This list is not intended to be complete, but instead to provide someone with reference material if they want to understand Scrum more thoroughly.

Resource	Description
Agile Software Development with Scrum, Ken Schwaber and Mike Beedle (Prentice Hall, 2001)	A thorough discussion of Scrum theory and practices. Gives the meat to the overview presented in Chapter 1 of this book.
www.controlchaos.com/	Ken Schwaber's Web site on Scrum.
jeffsutherland.com/	The codeveloper of Scrum's Web site. Jeff Sutherland provides various content related to software programming and technology, particularly objects, components, and Scrum. Very up-to-date and educational.
www.mountaingoatsoftware .com/scrum/	Mike Cohn's great Web site on Scrum.
www.scrumalliance.org	The home of the Certified ScrumMasters—those who are proficient in the use of Scrum.
www.agilealliance.org	The home of the AgileAlliance, with a great library of Agile and Scrum articles.
scrumdevelopment @eGroups.com	The home of the Scrum discussion group, with four years of discussion and hundreds of members.
www.xprogramming.com	Ron Jeffries's Web site about Scrum's brother, Extreme Programming (XP). XP provides many of the engineering practices that Scrum implements to ensure increments of potentially shippable product functionality.

Resource	Description
Process Dynamics, Modeling, and Control, Babatunde A. Ogunnaike and W. Harmon Ray (Oxford University Press, 1994)	The theory behind Scrum, first orally presented to me by Babatunde ("Tunde") at DuPont in 1995.
The Alphabet Versus the Goddess, Leonard Shlain (Viking Penguin, 1998)	Why all good ideas eventually become irrelevant, as they are codified and rationalized.
Wicked Problems, Righteous Solutions, Peter Degrace and Leslie Hulet Stahl (Yourdon Press, 1990)	A great book by the first people to call Scrum Scrum.
A Universe of Consciousness, Gerald Edelman (Basic Books, 2000)	A deep look at why it's so hard to turn requirements into working code.
Managing the Unknowable, Ralph D. Stacey (Josey-Bass, 1992)	One of the first presentations about the difficulties of managing complexity.
Complexity and Emergence in Organisations, Ralph D. Stacey (Routledge, 2000)	Providing a critique of the ways that complexity theory has been applied to understanding organizations and outining a new direction, this book calls for a radical reexamination of management thinking.
Artful Making, Rob Austin and Lee Devin (Prentice Hall, 2003)	An approach to managing creative work as adapted from the theater.

Appendix D

Fixed-Price, Fixed-Date Contracts

Tony is in charge of methodology development and deployment for a large professional services firm, EngageX. He and I have known each other for 10 years—ever since I licensed my company's process automation software to EngageX for automating its methodology. I was sure that Tony would want to hear about Scrum, so I called him and arranged for a meeting. Tony is one of the shrewdest people I know, and he quickly grasped the concepts and benefits of Scrum. But he wanted to know how Scrum addresses fixed-price, fixed-date contracts. These were the bread and butter of his firm, and the ability to estimate the contract and bring it in on schedule at or below cost was critical. His customers wanted to present a problem and have someone tell them exactly what the cost of solving it would be and when the solution would be delivered. In competitive situations, the firm with the best combination of reputation, low cost, and early date would get the business. Most of these customers had been burned more than once, and the trust required for collaboration between them and EngageX, or any other development organization or professional services firm, was unlikely, at least in the initial work.

I had to admit to Tony that I didn't know how to use Scrum to address his business. Scrum's principle is "the art of the possible," not "you give me what I paid for, when you said that you'd deliver it." For several years after my meeting with Tony, this problem rolled around in my head and just wouldn't go away, until finally I realized that Scrum had no silver bullet—it had to go about addressing fixed-price, fixed-date contracts exactly the way any other process would, including the defined, heavyweight methodologies. There simply was no way around analyzing the customer's requirements enough to understand the scope of the problem and designing enough to understand the number and complexity of the architecture and design artifacts. What a terrible realization! This meant adding a waterfall phase to the front of the Scrum methodology that would produce documentation. That was terrible, and what possible benefit could Scrum provide after it had been so corrupted?

The more I thought about it, the more I realized that—even though Scrum couldn't be used in its entirety—EngageX or any other organization bidding on fixed-price, fixed-date contracts could use Scrum to gain competitive advantage in bidding on fixed-price, fixed-date requests for proposals (RFPs). This approach could lead to collaboration between EngageX and its customers that would then lead those customers to see the benefits of Scrum. The approach is described below and has been used in several situations.

How to Gain Competitive Advantage

Most responses to RFPs consist of a bid, a date, qualifications, prior similar engagements, development methodology to be employed, and a plan, with the plan usually presented in high-level and low-level Gantt charts. The plan is a demonstration of the work to be performed, as well as a staffing and workload cost estimating mechanism. To derive this information, the prospect's RFP must be analyzed, with the requirements understood completely so that they can be decomposed into architectures and designs. When Scrum is used to bid on such a fixed-price, fixed-date RFP, these requirements would also be parsed into a new part of the bid, the Product Backlog. The Product Backlog would be used not only to show the prospect that all of the requirements were understood, but also to demonstrate that the bidding firm understood the priority of the requirements in generating value to the business. The most valuable requirements in solving the customer problems would be prioritized as high; the most irrelevant requirements would receive a low priority.

The firm making the bid would point out to the prospect that it had prepared a requirements list prioritized according to its assessment of the value and importance of the functionality to the prospect's business needs. The bidding firm could then tell the prospect that it did this because its development process was different from most other professional service firms. Rather than delivering the system all at once, it would build the system increment by increment. The firm liked to work this way so that the team working on the system could show the prospect what it had built every month to ensure that it was on track and meeting the prospect's needs. Every month, the firm's team would get together with the prospect and review the functionality it had just built.

The bidding firm would then point out that this had some potential side benefits to the prospect. Because it was turning only some requirements into business functionality, if the prospect wanted to change some of the lower priority requirements because of changing business conditions, the bidding firm would be able to handle this with minimum fuss. It wouldn't have put any effort into working on these later requirements, so nothing would be lost, nor would the prospect have spent any money on work that had not been performed.

As a concluding point, the bidding firm would also explain that its customers were often able to derive all of the business value they anticipated before all of the requirements were built. Following the 80/20 rule, many of its customers had been able to derive 80 percent of a project's value from just 20 percent of the functionality. The lowest priority requirements were often unnecessary frills. If the prospect engaged the bidding firm, it would give the prospect the option of canceling the work early when enough business value had been derived and prior to the contracted end date. There would be a penalty, of course, but it would be less than having the unnecessary requirements developed and implemented.

How to Ignore Competitive Advantage

These were all competitive advantages that a bidding firm employing Scrum could use to win a fixed-price, fixed-date RFP if the prospect was open to discussing them. Some prospects would be intrigued. Others might not even want to talk about it. Some wouldn't even know how to talk about it. At a U.S. Department of Defense workshop in 2002, I was part of a discussion about this approach. At the end of the discussion, a contracting officer for the U.S. Air Force said, "I don't even know what you people have been talking about. If you presented me with the type of stuff you've been describing, I'd call your bid out of compliance. Contracting officers in the Air Force and other services go through formal, rigorous training, and nothing in the training even hints at the things that you've been talking about." Using Scrum in fixed-price, fixed-date situations presents an opportunity, but only if your audience knows how to listen and is willing to listen.

Appendix E

Capability Maturity Model (CMM)

CMM is a framework that describes practices that an organization employs in developing software. CMM consists of five levels, numbered 1 through 5. Level 1 means that the organization doesn't have any defined, repeatable, or improvable approach to building software; basically, developers hack their way to a solution. At level 5, an organization has a defined, repeatable, and improvable set of practices for developing software. Level 1 is considered an immature organization; level 5 is considered a mature organization. At each level, the practices that should be employed are defined as key practice areas (KPAs). Bill Curtis and Mark Paulk from the Software Engineering Institute (SEI) at Carnegie Mellon University developed CMM in the early 1990s.

If an organization believes that it has thoroughly implemented the KPAs for a specific level, it can engage someone who has been certified by SEI to assess this. If the organization is compliant, it is so certified. Certification is a big deal, because some companies and governmental agencies won't hire any professional services firm that isn't certified to at least CMM level 3.

CMM at MegaFund

I introduced MegaFund in earlier chapters. MegaFund spent three years and over $40 million to improve its software development practices until it was certified at CMM level 3. At this level, MegaFund not only had a repeatable approach for managing any conceivable software development project, but it also had formally defined these practices. We looked at how MegaFund scaled a project to quickly support its entry into Web, telephone, and other advanced management of funds by its customers in Chapter 9.

Unfortunately for MegaFund, it had not defined practices that addressed a time-critical project that would automate ill-defined requirements on advanced and untried technologies like the project in Chapter 8. When MegaFund brought in Scrum for this project, the project had already been stalled for over nine months while team members tried unsuccessfully to jump the procedural and bureaucratic hurdles the CMM level 3 imposed on progress in unforeseen and undefined circumstances. I gained an unfavorable impression of CMM from this and later encounters with CMM implementations. However, as I was asked more frequently what I thought of CMM and how it related to Scrum, I realized that I needed more information and knowledge. To this end, I set up a meeting with Mark Paulk at SEI in the fall of 2002.

SEI, CMM, and Scrum

Mark was familiar with Extreme Programming, another Agile process similar to Scrum but more engineering focused and less management focused. However, he had only heard about Scrum. Throughout the first day, Mark taught me about CMM, and I taught Mark about Scrum. On my side, I was quite surprised and impressed by CMM. Mark related that it was only a framework describing an organization's maturity for developing software. How an organization satisfied that framework was up to the organization. Assessors were supposed to determine whether the manner in which the organization satisfied the framework was adequate. This enlightened me. Because almost every organization prior to 2001 used defined software development processes, CMM would of course build rigid, prescriptive, and defined methods for fleshing out the framework. These practices would suffer the weaknesses of all defined approaches—they would work only for situations that had been foreseen by those defining the practices. Since software development is a very complex process, there would be very few actual projects to which these practices would be applicable.

Mark then went over KPAs for the various levels with me. We then assessed how Scrum fulfilled the KPAs for each level. Mark was pleasantly surprised. Even though Scrum took an empirical approach, someone employing its practices would satisfy all of the CMM level 2 KPAs and many of the level 3 KPAs. The KPAs that weren't satisfied at level 3 were those that addressed institutionalizing the practices. These KPAs were addressed in 2003 when the Scrum Methodology, the Certified Scrum Program, and Project Quickstart were made available as products. Figure E-1 shows the degrees to which Scrum addresses the various KPAs in level 2 and level 3. A double check mark means fully compliant, and a single check mark means mostly compliant.

To see how Scrum's practices implement one of the KPAs, let's take a look at KPA 2, "Requirements management." The definition of this KPA is "The purpose of Requirements Management is to establish a common understanding between the customer and the software project of the customer's requirements that will be addressed by the software project." The Scrum mechanism for meeting this KPA is the Product Backlog, an openly visible listing of all functional and nonfunctional requirements maintained by the customers that is used to drive development, Sprint by Sprint. The emergent nature of the Product Backlog, with focus on only the top-priority items, maximizes the probability that investment in detailing requirements is of value. Lower-priority Product Backlog that might never be implemented is ignored until and unless it rises to the top of the Product Backlog list.

Level	Key Practice Area	Rating
2	Requirements management	✓✓
2	Software project planning	✓✓
2	Software project tracking and oversight	✓✓
2	Software subcontract management	
2	Software quality assurance	✓✓
2	Software configuration management	✓
3	Organization process focus	✓
3	Organization process definition	✓
3	Training program	✓
3	Integrated Software management	✓
3	Software product engineering	✓✓
3	Intergroup coordination	✓✓
3	Peer review	✓✓

Figure E-1   Scrum and CMM

This KPA is often interpreted as demanding *requirements traceability*, the ability to show how requirements are fulfilled in the delivered system. The manner in which Scrum addresses this interpretation is by demonstrating within 30 calendar days how every Product Backlog item that has been worked on during the Sprint operates as business functionality. The proof is through an actual demonstration of the functionality. As the customer accepts the functionality as complete, that completed item reduces the Product Backlog.

This completely empirical approach to requirements traceability fully meets the requirements of the KPA without extensive documentation or overhead to the development process. It also provides complete flexibility to manage and trace changes in requirements anytime throughout the project. Scrum addresses the rest of the KPAs for level 2 and 3 similarly, empirically and with a minimum of documentation and overhead.

Index

Ken Schwaber

Ken Schwaber codeveloped the Scrum process with Jeff Sutherland in the early 1990s and has used it ever since to help organizations struggling with complicated development projects. One of the signatories to the Agile Manifesto in 2001, he went on to found the AgileAlliance, of which he is currently the Chairman of the Board. Ken has over thirty years of experience in the various aspects of systems development.

Microsoft Press

Get step-by-step instruction *plus .NET* development software—*all in one box!*

Microsoft® Visual C#® .NET Deluxe Learning Edition— Version 2003
ISBN: 0-7356-1910-7
U.S.A. $119.99
Canada $173.99

Microsoft® Visual Basic® .NET Deluxe Learning Edition— Version 2003
ISBN: 0-7356-1906-9
U.S.A. $119.99
Canada $173.99

Microsoft® Visual C++® .NET Deluxe Learning Edition— Version 2003
ISBN: 0-7356-1908-5
U.S.A. $119.99
Canada $173.99

Everything you need to start developing powerful applications and services for Microsoft .NET is right here in three economical training packages. DELUXE LEARNING EDITIONS give you powerful Microsoft .NET development software— Visual C# .NET 2003 Standard, Visual Basic .NET 2003 Standard, and Visual C++ .NET 2003 Standard—along with Microsoft's popular Step by Step tutorials to help you learn the languages. Work at your own pace through easy-to-follow lessons and hands-on exercises. Then apply your new expertise to full development software — not simulations or trial versions. DELUXE LEARNING EDITIONS are the ideal combination of tools and tutelage for the Microsoft .NET Framework—straight from the source!

To learn more about the full line of Microsoft Press® products for developers, please visit us at:

microsoft.com/mspress/developer

Create awesome multimedia solutions **with code, tools, and tips from** Microsoft **Digital Media developers!**

Fundamentals of Programming the Microsoft® Windows Media® Platform
ISBN 0-7356-1911-5

Learn how to develop and deliver exceptional digital media solutions using the powerfully enhanced Windows Media 9 Series platform. Created by a technical expert on the Microsoft Windows Media team, this guide walks you through platform architecture and components—providing inside insights, real-world programming scenarios, automation techniques, and reusable code samples to help power your own streaming media solutions. You get step-by-step instructions on how to create applications to encode Windows Media files and streams, serve and receive audio and video streams, create customized players, and even build a complete broadcasting system—your own Internet radio station.

Fundamentals of Audio and Video Programming for Games
ISBN 0-7356-1945-X

Deliver console-rocking sound, music, and video effects to your games with this all-in-one toolkit for C++ game programmers. Load the CD—and experience Microsoft's Digital Media developers at play, learning how to use Microsoft DirectX® 9 technologies to produce amazing, professional-quality effects. From mixing and moving sounds around a 3-D space to taking video to the third dimension, you get expert insights and performance tips direct from the developers, along with a game-ready arsenal of code, copyright-free audio and video, and ready-to-use effects on CD. It's everything you need to fuel your creativity—and take your game players to spectacular new 3-D worlds!

Microsoft Press has many other titles to help you put development tools and technologies to work.
To learn more about the full line of Microsoft Press® products for developers, please visit:

microsoft.com/mspress/developer

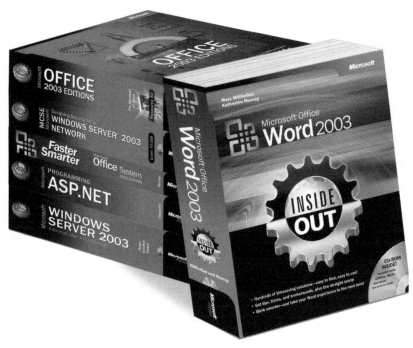

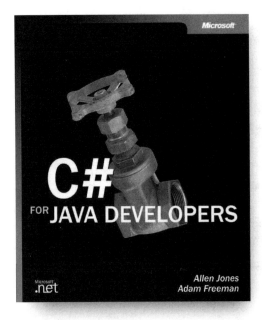